Multiple Intelligences

in practice

enhancing self-esteem and learning in the classroom

Mike Fleetham

Published by
Network Continuum Education
PO Box 635, Stafford ST16 1BF

An imprint of The Continuum International Publishing Group Ltd

First published 2006
© Mike Fleetham 2006

ISBN-13: 978 1 85539 141 3
ISBN-10: 1 85539 141 4

The right of Mike Fleetham to be identified as the author of this work has been asserted in accordance with Sections 77 and 78 of the Copyright, Designs and Patents Act 1988.

Acknowledgements
The publishers would like to thank the following for permission to use extracts from their material in this book. Every effort has been made to contact copyright holders of material produced in this book. The publishers apologize for any omissions and will be pleased to rectify them at the earliest opportunity.

Association for Supervision and Curriculum Development for the extract on page 46 from *Becoming a Multiple Intelligences School* by Tom Hoerr, 2000. Reprinted by permission

Basic Books, a member of Perseus Books LLC, for extracts on pages 17 (repeated 19), 38, 48 and 66 from *Intelligence Reframed* by Howard Gardner, Copyright © 1999 Howard Gardner. Reprinted by permission

Professor Áine Hyland for the abridged extract on page 21 from 'Multiple Intelligences, Curriculum and Assessment Project, Final Report', University College Cork, 2000

The Random House Group for the extract on page 16 from *The Curious Incident of the Dog in the Night-Time* by Mark Haddon, published by Jonathan Cape. Reprinted by permission

Branton Shearer for the MIDAS profile on page 60. Author: C. Branton Shearer, PhD, *The MIDAS Professional Manual*, MI Research and Consulting, Inc. www.miresearch.org

Teachers College Press for extracts on pages 87, 100 and 109 from *Multiple Intelligences in the Elementary Classroom: A Teacher's Toolkit* by Susan Baum, Julie Viens and Barbara Slatin

Editor:	Roanne Charles
Design by:	Neil Hawkins, Network Continuum Education
Cover design by:	Network Continuum Education
Illustrations by:	Kate Sheppard
Proofreader:	Lynn Bresler
Indexer:	Sue Lightfoot

Printed in Great Britain by MPG Books Ltd, Bodmin, Cornwall

Contents

Author's acknowledgements

I would like to thank the following three people for, respectively, support, encouragement and the opportunity to develop my work with multiple intelligences:

Rick Barnes, Portsmouth LEA (2000)
Sue Davies and Sandra Lawlor, Fernhurst Junior School, Portsmouth (2000).

'Teachers affect eternity, and they rarely know it.' Thanks to my tutors from University College Chichester who sowed the 'MI seed' in my brain in 1993.

Many children and educators have contributed to this book in lots of different ways, including case studies, advice and inspiration. Their willingness to take calculated risks with learning is very much appreciated:

Class 3F (2000), Fernhurst Junior School, Portsmouth
Class 4F (2001), Paulsgrove Primary School, Portsmouth
Natalie Earl, Craneswater Junior School, Southsea
Dr Branton Shearer, MI Research and Consulting, Ohio
Dr Tom Hoerr, New City School, St Louis
Maria Penicud and Angela Mumford, Arbour Vale Special School, Slough
Sean and Fiona, Aspire, Angus Council
Cheryl Garlinge, Baylis Court School, Slough
Rebecca Nelson, Beeston County Primary School, Beeston
Mary Sefton, Bracknell Forest LEA
Debbie Anderson and Vicki Cleeve, College Park Infant School, Southsea
Liz Flaherty, Cove Secondary School, Farnborough
Tina, Barbie and Davina, Front Lawn Junior School, Havant
Jo Iles, Gillotts School, Henley-on-Thames
Alison Spittles, Goldsmith Infant School, Southsea
Sue Harden-Davies, Mayville High School, Southsea
Trish Raper, Milton Cross Secondary School, Portsmouth
Andrew Cowell, Oakwood School, West Sussex
Sue Harris and Elspeth Simpson, Pinewood Infant School, Farnborough
Anne Cassidy, Portsmouth Family Learning
Chris Neanon, Portmouth University
Caroline Freestone, St Michael's School, Doncaster
Louise Rich, Wallisdean Junior School, Fareham.

It takes a wide range of intelligences to produce a book – thanks to the following experts for sharing theirs as a collaborative group:

Bridget, Lily, Neil, Marc and Jim at Network Continuum (visual, linguistic, intrapersonal, interpersonal and logical); Roanne for her incisive editing (intrapersonal, interpersonal, linguistic, logical); Kate for illustrations (visual, kinesthetic); and Terry for wise visual advice and cunning interpretations of MI concepts (visual, existential, linguistic).

Apologies if anyone's work or acknowledgement has been either omitted or edited – all contributions in whatever form have been greatly valued.

This book is dedicated to my wife and favourite person, Lucy

Foreword

Even before Howard Gardner's conceptualization of the theory of multiple intelligences (MI), good teachers knew that students had many different strengths and ways of learning. Those good teachers modified their curriculum and teaching as they were able, but it was all done rather intuitively. Gardner changed how we view intelligence and how we look at children; but he did not provide a strategy for bringing MI to life.

In the nearly 25 years since Gardner's *Frames of Mind* was published, many educators and authors have taken their hand to providing tools and strategies for teachers. Still, there often remain many questions about implementing MI. *MI in Practice* will definitely help to fill that void. It is an excellent compendium of theory, practice, reflection, suggestions and anecdotes.

In these pages, a teacher shares her experiences of using MI for an entire school year, and other teachers offer case studies. I came away wanting to meet these teachers and wanting to share their ideas with my faculty members. Their experiences, coupled with Mike's creativity and encompassing view of MI, create a wonderful resource.

Mike notes that his pupils referred to him as 'intelligence man', and after reading this book, it is easy to see why. Mike not only understands MI, and how it can be used to help students and teachers succeed, he lives MI. By that, I mean that he clearly recognizes that we are all unique, and he reflects that appreciation in his attitudes and practices. His approach is not prescriptive in any way but filled with suggestions for how to work with students and their parents.

To be fair, Mike also recognizes the realities that teachers face each day. Children don't always come to school ready to learn; parents aren't always supportive and understanding; school administrators can be rigid and critical. And, oh yes, the government seems overly focused on percentiles. Given this context, implementing MI can be a challenge. Yet it is precisely because of this context that MI can be such a wonderful tool. MI is not a panacea, but it can bring life and success to every classroom.

This book demystifies both what MI is and how it can be used. It provides concrete examples and, at the same time, serves as a bit of a cheerleader for the reader. A practising educator, Mike knows that it is harder to 'do' MI than to describe it. These pages are full of examples, some self-effacing humour and lots of encouragement. Perhaps Mike's attitude can be summed up in his statement, MI is 'your potential to think, act, solve problems and create valuable things in eight and a half (nine) different, equally valuable ways' (page 35). As set out in this book, MI is more than an add-on or something to be done this week or this month; rather, MI becomes a new way to look at learners, to think about teaching and to reflect on our profession.

Tom Hoerr

Tom Hoerr is the Head of the New City School in St Louis, USA, where multiple intelligences theory has been implemented since 1988. He is the author of *Becoming a Multiple Intelligences School* and *The Art of School Leadership* (both ASCD). He can be contacted at trhoerr@newcityschool.org.

A word about MI in education

'The single most important contribution education can make to a child's development is to help him towards a field where his talents best suit him, where he will be satisfied and competent. We've completely lost sight of that. Instead we subject everyone to an education where, if you succeed, you will be best suited to be a college professor. And we evaluate everyone along the way according to whether they meet that narrow standard of success. We should spend less time ranking children and more time helping them to identify their natural competencies and gifts and cultivate those. There are hundreds and hundreds of ways to succeed and many many different abilities that will help you get there.'

Howard Gardner

Introduction

I have written this book for educators who want to infuse multiple intelligences (MI) theory into their teaching. It includes lots of practical ideas and case studies demonstrating successful implementation. It shows you how teachers are using MI theory to enhance many aspects of teaching and learning – planning, assessment, creativity and thinking. It then gives you the tools to do the same yourself.

The ideas and case studies have mainly come from experience with school-age learners (4–16 years), but they are easily adapted for older (or younger) ones. Once you have grasped MI theory, you begin to see any learner, or any learning, in a richer way.

MI is not an educational bolt-on or quick fix. It is not a curriculum, strategy or a catch-up programme. Nor is it a trendy educational 'gadget' – here today, gone tomorrow. MI is a scientifically validated philosophy that has been steadily absorbed into classrooms worldwide over the last 20 years.

MI offers an enriched way of seeing the world that can expand your thinking about human success. It gives you the chance to discover, value and enhance the talents of all learners, not just those who are suited to 'traditional' schooling. And it provides a means to improve self-esteem, self-motivation and independence, which can then lead to raised academic standards and life success.

This book doesn't aim to tell you how you should use the theory of multiple intelligences, or even try to prove to you that it 'works'. That would be against the spirit of MI. But it does present the basics of the theory and how it can be brought to life in the classroom. The book offers a menu rather than a diet. This means choices of really practical stuff: classroom resources, activities and ideas for you to apply, adapt, evaluate, praise, criticize, or even discard, as you wish! You are a creative, professional educator and only you know what is best for yourself and your learners.

Section 1: Discovering MI looks at intelligence in general, then goes on to explain the theory of multiple intelligences in an accessible way. There are some activities to try as you read, which can be repeated later with your learners.

Section 2: Using MI presents many ways in which teachers have made multiple intelligences their own, and suggests how you can begin to use it in your lessons. It demonstrates the benefits of using MI. The section offers advice on how to carry out MI profiling and how to set up an MI classroom, and it introduces four different approaches to MI teaching and learning:

- Building on strengths
- Developing talents
- Enhancing understanding
- Solving problems.

At the back of the book are suggestions for materials and resources that will take your MI learning further.

MI is a powerful and empowering tool, but it needs a skilled person to pick it up and make something valuable with it: you're that person… and the valuable thing you're making…? The teaching that your learners really need!

Oh, and here's another very good reason for reading on:

'1. States Parties agree that the education of the child shall be directed to: (a) The development of the child's personality, talents and mental and physical abilities to their fullest potential.'

Article 29, United Nations Convention on the Rights of the Child

…Multiple intelligences can help you to do just that!

Discovering MI

Personalizing learning

It was a lovely hot summer's day, but the animals of the forest were not happy. Lion had been having ideas again. His latest was this – that everyone had to pass a test before they were allowed to drink from the pool. The pool had been drying up and there wasn't enough water to go round.

None of the animals knew what Lion's test was, but they all started getting ready anyway. Snake was good at curling round things and fitting into small holes, so she slithered off into the undergrowth to practise.

Monkey could climb trees and make lots of noise, so he swung off, chattering loudly to himself.

Elephant could squeeze things and was great at trumpeting with his trunk. So he found a few smaller animals, held them carefully under his foot, and gave them a loud blast with his trunk. (Don't worry, the little animals were only slightly dazed!)

Anteater burrowed her nose into a huge anthill and tried a new technique she'd been working on – the multiple slurp.

Just then, Lion loped up. All the other animals stopped what they were doing as he opened his mouth to speak.

'Animals of the forest, the summer is hot, water is scarce, the pool is drying up. Only those of you who pass my test will be allowed anywhere near it.'

'We knew that,' they thought, collectively.

'But what's the test please?' they asked

'All you have to do,' said Lion, 'is squash a pineapple.'

Elephant looked happy, while all the other animals had long and thirsty faces.

It's really easy to squash a pineapple if you're an elephant. It's not so straightforward should you happen to be a snake... Maybe a boa constrictor could have a crack at it, but generally snakes get an E in squashing. Likewise, it's easy to sail through school if you excel in timed, written tests. It's not so straightforward if you happen to prefer showing what you know in more practical ways – talking, painting, singing, acting; through video, photography or audio recordings.

Teachers have always known that children shine in many different ways. The writers, the talkers, the singers, the friendly ones, the thinkers and the doers – they all make themselves known early on in a school year. And this diversity should be each child's strength – not a burden to carry.

Unique skills and talents should be discovered, valued and brought to bear on learning: if a child has strong visual skills, then surely he should be able to exhibit what he knows using these skills? If a child has great musical talent, surely she should have the chance to use this to express her learning?

In this section of the book, multiple intelligences theory is introduced as a method to do just this. It discusses different ways of defining intelligence and shows how MI integrates well with more traditional views of 'being clever'. A light-hearted yet thorough introduction to the theory then follows, during which it should become clear just how powerful MI is when describing each learner's achievements and potential.

Every Child Matters

As I write, two big things in UK education are the *Every Child Matters* initiative and, as part of this, 'personalized learning'. Like most big things in education there are passionate advocates, fierce opponents, people selling resources and training, and practitioners like you and I who have to implement other people's grand ideas.

Every Child Matters is a very worthy attempt to ensure that each child in the country is kept safe and healthy, can reach their full potential through education, and then eventually can become a valuable member of society. This will happen as the various agencies that work with children begin to communicate with each other more effectively.

Personalized learning is a key strand of this. Note that there are subtle, but important differences in the phrases used around personalized learning: 'personalizing for...' and 'personalizing by...'. The 'for' bit means teachers do the personalizing, the 'by' is when learners do it themselves. By now, Ofsted will be on the hunt for schools where learning is genuinely personalized by the learners not by the teachers. I wonder if personalized inspections are around the corner – where the inspection is adapted to meet the needs of the school?

For details, visit www.everychildmatters.gov.uk/ete/personalisedlearning, or see *Personalising learning: Next steps in working laterally* by David Hargreaves (iNet).

Personalized learning is a broad term, but the key to 'doing it' is quite specific. To personalize learning, you must understand the learner – how they learn best, what makes them tick, what motivates them; who they are. Multiple intelligences can play a big role in this. It's a very powerful way to portray a learner – it describes their skills, potential and preferences. It suggests how they will learn best by defining the activities that suit their talents. MI gives students a voice and it gives them a choice in their learning.

But there are other aspects to personalizing learning – how does MI fit in?

MI, thinking skills and learning styles

Three concepts that keep cropping up in educational debates and newspaper columns are:

- learning styles
- thinking skills
- multiple intelligences.

Together, they describe the learning process, but they often get confused. This might help you to tell them apart:

Learning styles are the different ways in which a learner takes in information.

Thinking skills are the different ways in which a learner processes, stores and retrieves information.

Multiple intelligences are the different skills and talents a learner uses to make products and solve problems – to demonstrate learning.

The boundaries between all three are very fuzzy, but one way to represent them is like this:

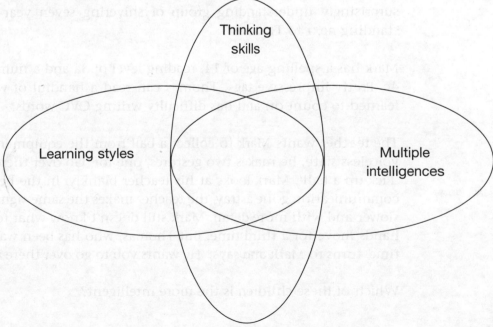

Learning styles tend towards the 'front end' of learning; thinking skills towards the middle; and multiple intelligences the back end, though each one does contain features of the other. For example:

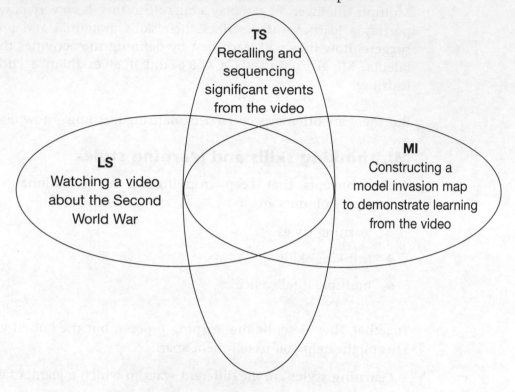

The main point is that, although they do have features in common, learning styles are different from multiple intelligences.

What is intelligence?

It is a Monday morning in late autumn. The Year 3 class is timetabled for PE. It is cold out on the playground. The teacher has struggled into school with a sore throat and a headache. He is using hand signals to direct a surprisingly understanding group of shivering seven year olds. Mark is standing next to Thomas.

Mark has a spelling age of 14, reading level of 3a and a numeracy score of 4c. Pretty impressive tags. Thomas can read a handful of words, has just learned to count on and has difficulty writing CVC words.

The teacher wants Mark to collect a ball from the equipment store. In his voiceless state, he makes two gestures, one for 'Go over there', another for 'Pick up a ball'. Mark looks at his teacher blankly. In the best tradition of communication gone astray, the teacher makes the same signals again, only slower and with more detail. Mark still doesn't know what to do when the hands move for a third time. But Thomas, who has been watching all this time, turns to Mark and says, 'He wants you to go over there and get a ball.'

Which of these children is the more intelligent?

And, on a scale from 1 to 10, how clever are you? After a little think, mark it here:

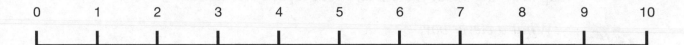

Addle-pated or enlightened?

The *Oxford Thesaurus of English* lists over 80 words for 'stupid'. However, it includes only 31 for 'intelligent'. That means you have a lot more choice of things to mutter under your breath when you lock yourself out of your house, compared to when you correctly answer all the questions on *Who Wants to be a Millionaire?*. If you have a thesaurus to hand, try the following. Marvel at the variety the English language offers you!

ACTIVITY

Alone: Research words for 'intelligent' and words for 'stupid'. There are some to start you off below. When you've collected a list, sort them into ascending order. For example, which of these implies more intelligence: 'wise' or 'quick-witted'? Which word suggests more stupidity: 'dull' or 'empty-headed'?

With your learners: Spice up the research a bit by including slang and dialect – including playground vernacular. Remember to set reasonable limits of decency and forbid any negative personal comments between the children.

bovine   thick   dense   empty-headed   bird-brained

dull   clever   keen   smart   addle-pated

enlightened   canny   senseless   sharp

moronic   gifted   idiotic   genius

slow   sensible   brainy   witless   knowing

bright   capable   talentless   ignorant   unintelligent

Words like this are often used without considering their meaning or impact. If you say that someone is 'smart', what do you mean? Are they good at maths or languages? Can they pass exams? Are they successful – wealthy, healthy, happy; own a fast car, a large house? Then if someone has been 'stupid', have they made a mistake? Been too slow in answering? Forgotten something? Not used their common sense? Failed? Or just never knew something? If you are called any of the following, what do you end up believing about yourself and your capacity for success?

'What a clever boy!'

'You are so stupid!'

'You're really brainy you know.'

'You're one sandwich short of a picnic.'

Of course, as teachers we don't now use words or labels that criticize our learners' intellectual capacity and potential to succeed – at least not in front of them. But what do we think and believe about this idea of 'intelligence'? Are we evaluating learners on a scale from Genius to Dullard without knowing what the scale really means? The *Oxford English Dictionary* doesn't help much:

'Intelligent – having or showing intelligence; quick of mind, clever.'

Yet there are those people who have been unfairly labelled as 'stupid' but who are very successful – David Beckham for example. And we all know a Beckham – a friend, relative or colleague who is very successful despite having no GCSEs or being dyslexic. Consider these school report comments:

'Certainly on the road to failure... hopeless... rather a clown in class... wasting other pupils' time.'

1957 report for John Lennon (age 17), musician

'...though her written work is the product of an obviously lively imagination, it is a pity that her spelling derives from the same source.'

1943 report for Beryl Bainbridge (age 9), author

I wonder if your own school reports said similar things? Or worse! Mine usually pointed out careless spelling and tatty handwriting. In the first year of secondary school, our form tutor asked us to write down our hobbies. I noted one of mine as 'being inteligent'. This calculated risk was displayed on the board for all to see and my spelling mistake waved in front of me for days to come. Crushed, I sank into a bout of pre-teen angst – my linguistic slip-up had labelled me as stupid.

Many years later (the angst now mostly gone), while snoozing in a psychology lecture, my ears pricked up to the presenter's throwaway comment, '...and there's even a guy in America who reckons there are seven different ways to be intelligent.' He was referring to Professor Howard Gardner and his theory of multiple intelligences.

It's a powerful theory, proposing that there are many ways to be clever and that every one of us is intelligent in our own unique way. No longer, it says, is intelligence reserved for those with a high IQ score, or good spelling, or the ability to remember their front door keys.

Deep in conversation at a party, you will usually pick out your name from the buzz and chatter, even if it's said at the other side of the room. You're programmed for it. I do the same with 'intelligent', 'stupid' and their synonyms. Whenever I hear an 'intelligence word' I note it and think about what the speaker really means. I should probably find a better hobby, but it does give an insight into what people believe about intelligence. For example:

On the bus: 'Sit down, you silly boy!'

In the pub: 'Rooney – yeah, the lad's a genius.'

In the playground: 'She's not too bright, but she's really good at art and design.'

In a department store: 'Am I thick or something? How do I find my way to bedroom furnishings?'

Experts will always argue about the definition of intelligence, but us lay people have some pretty fascinating insights too. Before you turn the page to see what some people have suggested, try this short exercise. In no more than two sentences, complete the following in your own words:

Intelligence is...

_____
_____
_____
_____
_____
_____
_____
_____
_____
_____

Here are some thoughts about intelligence from a wide range of people – young and old, famous and fictional, expert and layperson. How do they compare to what you thought?

Intelligence is very useful... but often elusive.

Alan Titchmarsh, gardener and author

Intelligence is the ability to encode, evaluate and utilize a large amount of novel information very quickly.

Professor Mary Phillips, neuroscientist

The ability to speak does not make you intelligent.

Qui-Gon Jinn to Jar Jar Binks in *Star Wars: The Phantom Menace*

Mr Jeavons said that I was a very clever boy. I said that I wasn't clever. I was just noticing how things were, and that wasn't clever. That was being observant. Being clever was when you looked at how things were and used the evidence to work out something new. Like the universe expanding, or who committed a murder.

Christopher Boone in *The Curious Incident of the Dog in the Night-Time*, by Mark Haddon

Being intelligent and smart, well that's one thing – money in the bank!

Anne Robinson, TV presenter

Intelligence is being good at something.

Cameron, Year 4 pupil

Intelligence is too big and amorphous to define in a box.

Philip Pullman, author (on a worksheet with a box in which to write his answer)

Intelligence is seeing one thing in terms of another: Sir McFarlane Burnett in 1959 realized that the principles of Darwinian evolution could be imported into a completely different domain, the immune system.

Professor Susan Greenfield, scientist

Intelligence is the ability to be happy.

Vicky, web designer

Intelligence is what the intelligence tests test.

Professor E.G. Boring, psychologist

I haven't got any so I can't really say what it is.

Brian, retired LEA adviser

Intelligence is creating solutions.

Lucy, mathematician

Intelligence is engaging brain before mouth.

Anonymous secondary schoolteacher

Intelligence is a biopsychological potential to process information that can be activated in a cultural setting to solve problems or create products that are of value in a culture.

Professor Howard Gardner

Intelligence is seeing the connections among seemingly disparate pieces of information as a means of understanding the bigger picture.

Professor Sir Peter Crane, Director, Royal Botanic Gardens, Kew

If people never did silly things, nothing intelligent would ever get done.

Ludwig Wittgenstein, philosopher

The word 'genius' isn't applicable to football. A genius is a guy like Norman Einstein.

Joe Theisman, NFL football quarterback and sports analyst

Intelligence is an indefinable quality which can not be defined.

Nigel, solicitor

MI, IQ and g

Present-day Western understanding and evaluation of intelligence can be traced back to the beginning of the twentieth century. In the early 1900s, Alfred Binet, a well-intentioned French psychologist, developed a written test of intelligence. Through a series of questions, he wanted to establish whether children were at risk of failure in school, so that the authorities could give them appropriate support.

Then, in 1912, German psychologist Wilhelm Stern developed Binet's work and gave us two letters that have been burned into the skin of intelligence ever since: IQ. He rationalized test results into the Intelligence Quotient: the ratio of a person's mental age to their chronological age. The final figure is multiplied by 100 to produce the IQ score. So, an IQ of 100 means that you are as bright as could be expected for your age. Anything over 100 and you feel very good about yourself, anything below and there's obviously something wrong with the test questions.

The items in an IQ test measure only a limited set of human talents, including verbal reasoning, numerical reasoning, visual thinking and logical problem solving. The Wechsler Adult Intelligence Scale, version III (WAIS-III) is an expanded version that produces a measure called 'g', or 'general intelligence'. It assesses 13 mental faculties such as arithmetic, sequencing, vocabulary and processing speed, but still has limitations.

Both IQ and g are the results of psychometric tests. Since 1912, loads of people have taken them and they have generated a huge amount of data. Some interesting questions have emerged: How do genes and environment effect intelligence? How does intelligence change with age? Are factors of gender, race and culture reflected in intelligence scores? Does the intelligence of the people in a country change over time? Is intelligence actually that important?

But all of this is based on an arbitrary and restricted set of criteria. Who chose and gave value to the components in the intelligence tests? Who decided which human abilities should be included or left out? And what are the consequences of making these choices? It could be argued that by restricting the range of skills measured in an intelligence test, we are denying 'intelligence' and then possibly 'success' to a great number of people; people who just happen to have skills that are equally valuable but not present on the test paper.

Just like a SAT paper, the IQ test produces a single number that defines the person who sat the test and can be used to sum up their potential.

Society adopted (and still values) IQ because it measures things that society values. And it's very easy to understand – the higher the number, the higher the intelligence (or at least, the more test questions answered correctly). Such a straightforward measure has its place – IQ measures a valuable set of skills. But it is a narrow set, and if society's view of 'intelligence' is to expand to include all skills and talents, then society must learn to value all skills and talents equally.

For more background on IQ and g, see *Intelligence – A Very Short Introduction* by Ian J. Deary (OUP).

The theory of multiple intelligences is an intriguing expansion of the concept of intelligence. Put simply, it states that there are many ways to be intelligent, not just by scoring highly in a psychometric test. Harvard psychologist Howard Gardner first presented his idea in 1983 after working with brain-damaged patients.

He had noticed that damage to specific brain regions affected only certain skills in his patients, leaving others intact. He proposed that many different 'kinds of minds' had evolved within the human brain, each of these minds being endowed with a separate intelligence. He went further and argued that each separate intelligence was equally valuable. In *Intelligence Reframed*, Gardner defines an intelligence as:

'A biopsychological potential to process information that can be activated in a cultural setting to solve problems or create products that are of value in a culture.'

Intelligence is your ability to do things that other people value. It's the origin of your skills and talents; the manifestation in the real world of your hidden brain processes – your thoughts turned into actions. It then follows that if all of your brain is present and intact (teachers in the last week of summer term may feel theirs are not), then you have all of the intelligences, to varying degrees, each being of equal worth. For example, a child who has incredible ball-control skills and can manipulate the tiniest of objects with patience has a strong bodily intelligence. She would be making great use of the brain regions controlling movement. This is on a par with another child who communicates well and has a highly developed linguistic intelligence – and is using the brain's language centres. A rugby player sending a drop kick over the bar draws on bodily, visual and intrapersonal intelligence.

If we value each part of our brain equally then surely the skills and talents produced by each part are equally valuable? A gymnastics sequence is as valuable as an essay; a painting as worthy as a solved equation.

This concept is often seen as a serious challenge to the intelligence establishment – especially by some people with very high IQs; but it needn't be. If you look more closely, there's actually no conflict between MI and IQ. It's not one or the other, but both. IQ is a measure of certain skills, all of which are included in MI. It's like looking through the lens of a camera – the shot you take is IQ, and the whole 360-degree panorama in which you are standing is MI.

The theory of multiple intelligences has been jeered as popular pseudo-science. But it has also been cheered by those who want a theory to back up their belief in the full range of human talents. Howard Gardner is scrupulous with his scientific definition of an intelligence. Each one must meet eight criteria, one of which (ironically) is that psychometric evidence supports its existence.

In fact, Gardner took around ten years to add the eighth intelligence (naturalist) to his original seven, and has recently been looking into a ninth: existential. Currently, existential intelligence is awarded the status of a 'half intelligence'. This is not meant to devalue existential talents. It merely points out that there is not, as yet, enough evidence against the eight criteria. (See pages 23–35 for explanations of the intelligences, and pages 39–40 for the eight criteria.)

There are many other theories of intelligence and even other concepts of multiple intelligences. We can find value in all of them. However, different ways of seeing have different results. For example, if you choose to see intelligence in only the IQ score, then intelligence will be bestowed only on a certain few. If you choose to see intelligence sweeping over the whole range of human talents, then everyone is clever. Instead of asking, 'How clever are you?' (IQ), we now ask, 'How are you clever?' (MI) – a tiny difference with far-reaching consequences. It is your choice, and the choice of everyone else in our culture, to decide what is and what is not a valuable skill or talent; to decide who is and who is not clever.

Let's look at how some different cultures value intelligences...

How you shape intelligence

An Englishman, an Irishman and a Scotsman walk into a bar. The barman takes one look at them and says, 'Is this some sort of joke?'

The Irish have long been the butt of many English jokes – just as Texans are for other Americans and Turks for Greeks. Here we look at just how inaccurate this is.

Professor Áine Hyland of University College Cork carried out a major research project between 1995 and 1999 into Gardner's multiple intelligences. Working with Irish primary and secondary teachers, she investigated the implications of MI for curriculum and assessment.

Her final project report ('Multiple Intelligences, Curriculum and Assessment') includes a summary of intelligence, multiple intelligences and the whole intelligence debate. It also includes a section, part of which is included on the next page, which really opened up my own thinking about these issues and how language and culture shape our understanding of intelligence.

'Given the diversity of views as to what might constitute intelligence in Ireland, it is not surprising that there is no one word for intelligence in the Irish language... "Eirimiúil" is probably the word that most closely approximates the English word "intelligent" but it is not often used, and rarely within a schooling context. The word "cliste" is probably most often used to denote intelligence or cleverness. "Duine cliste" is a "clever" person – clever with positive connotations and not confined to academic learning. It can encompass creativity, talent and skills in a wide range of areas. "Duine glic", on the other hand, is also a clever person, but usually intelligent in pursuit of their own interests... "Duine críonna" is a wise or sagacious person – worldly wise from the experience of many years... Yet another word that implies intelligence in the Irish language is "stuama". "Duine stuama" is solid, reliable and sensible – an important form of intelligence in certain situations. In addition to the above words, modern dictionary translations of "intelligent" include "intleachtúil" (derived from the English word intellectual) and "tuisceanach" (which translated directly means "understanding").'

Professor Hyland's explanation shows clearly how 'intelligence' can be much broader than IQ. In Ireland, a range of words is used to describe the variety of talents esteemed by the Irish people. It demonstrates how a group can evolve unique ideas about being clever based on the skills most valued by the people in the group: you're smart if you can do the valuable things.

If you lived in a land where food fell from the sky when you danced, dancers would be the clever ones; if you were from a species with no sight or hearing, your skills of touch would define your intelligence; and if you inhabited a country where seven year olds were given exams in maths, language and science, then the ones with the highest scores would be the brainiest. What a place that would be...

Irish speakers are free to be clever in a whole range of ways and Professor Hyland suggests an intriguing reason for this: an IQ test that could be administered in the Irish language was never developed – the Irish people have never been saddled with IQ scores!

All cultures have their 'Irish', as indicated by the following alternative tale. Feel free to customize it: Turkish academics could be Ofsted inspectors; Greeks could be headteachers...

Three Greek and three Turkish academics are travelling to a conference on multiple intelligences. At the train station, the three Turks each buy one-way tickets and watch as the Greeks buy only one one-way ticket between them.

'How are three people going to travel on only one ticket?' asks one Turk.

'Watch and you'll see,' answers one Greek.

They all board the train. The Turks take their seats but all three Greeks cram into a toilet and close the door behind them. Shortly after the train has departed, the conductor comes around. He knocks on the toilet door and says, 'Ticket, please.'

The door opens just a crack and a single arm emerges with a ticket in hand. The conductor checks the ticket and moves on.

The Turks see this and agree it is quite a clever idea.

After the conference, the Turks buy just one ticket for the return trip. To their astonishment, the Greeks don't buy a ticket at all.

'How are you going to travel without a ticket?' asks one perplexed Turk.

'Watch and you'll see,' answers a Greek.

When they board the train the three Turks cram into a toilet and the three Greeks cram into another one nearby. The train departs. Shortly afterwards, one of the Greeks leaves his toilet and walks to the toilet where the Turks are hiding. He knocks on the door and says, 'Ticket, please.'

Eight and a half ways to be clever

A few months ago my wife and I took a trip to a large furniture store. Having installed our children in the crèche, my wife and I began 30 minutes of frantic browsing. (Browsing frantically *is* possible – it's in the parents' manual!)

I like maps, so I thought we could use the store's floor plans to get about effectively. There are paths, weaving through beds, plants, fabrics and computer tables. There are also secret short cuts to the café and escalators. I head off confidently, but after a while my sense of direction has disappeared and I've lost my understanding of where things are in relation to other things.

Several days later – it seemed – we emerged, blinking into the bright morning sun and loaded our newly purchased flat-pack wardrobe into the car.

At home, after five hours of 'easy self-assembly' and unsuccessful attempts to follow the instructions, my daughter explained that the wardrobe would 'fit together in a less wobbly way if you move that bit over there, so it looks like that drawing on the paper.' My daughter has a rich imagination and can manipulate pictures easily in her head.

This episode introduces aspects of one of the intelligences – the **visual/spatial** intelligence. You need its skills to successfully shop in furniture stores. Firstly, map reading to get to your nearest store, then parking – manoeuvring your car into a tight space, respectfully leaving neighbouring cars undamaged. Once in the store it's helpful to have a visual memory of the positions of the different departments – so you can rush back from the checkout to pick up a bathroom mirror. Then, making the furniture 'look like that drawing on the paper' requires visual (and actual) manipulation of a large number of pieces, relating them to the diagrams in the usually word-free instructions.

Visual/spatial intelligence

Your potential to think in images and to understand how objects fit and move together in the real world.

It's to do with seeing things and being able to recall, change and express what you see. This could be anything from taking a photograph, to painting a favourite memory or daydream. It's also about knowing how things fit together and how they move in relation to each other – using a map, assembling or arranging furniture, remembering where you parked your car.

ACTIVITY

Alone: Take a journey in your mind: Start from the place where you are now, and, without actually moving, take yourself to your kitchen – use your imagination. If you are already in your kitchen, travel to someone else's. It may help to close your eyes. Be aware of the journey. How much detail do you see? If you're not at home, what was the traffic like getting there?

With your learners: Guide them on imaginary visual journeys linked to curriculum content, for example back in time via historical milestones; around the local community; around your classroom displays; along a number line; around a set of 2D or 3D shapes.

For more technical information about visual intelligence, try *Visual Intelligence: How We Create What We See* by Donald D. Hoffman (W.W. Norton & Co).

So far, Howard Gardner acknowledges eight and a half intelligences. We've bought a flat-pack wardrobe with our visual/spatial intelligence, so let's try our other intelligences in different shops. The shops certainly don't tell the full story of skills and talents and each shop can represent many intelligences, but the obvious shops can be a starting point to bring the theory of MI to life. So, let's carry on shopping!

Music store

Whatever your musical taste, there's probably something in the CD racks here that you would enjoy: rock, pop, classical, jazz, R&B, folk, world music...

I walk in, attracted by the music that's playing, and suddenly a different set of brain areas spring to life. I'm thinking music: I'm hearing drums, strings, horns, synthesizers, singing; I'm picking out the rhythm, melody, harmony and the 'feeling' of the music. I love the track and I know why: I love the rhythm; the melody is engaging and changes unexpectedly; the hypnotic string riff makes the hairs on the back of my neck stand on end.

I'm using part of my **musical/rhythmic** intelligence. This is the intelligence that helped me struggle through piano lessons from the age of seven; the one that produced some of the horrendous noises made in a series of sixth form and university bands; the one that responded to voice training lessons and learned to sing properly; and the one that enjoys exploring and appreciating the fascinating world of music.

I think about explaining all this to the girl behind the counter, but she seems preoccupied with the boy behind the counter, so I just buy the CD and leave.

Musical/rhythmic intelligence

Your potential to think in sounds and to understand how music is made, performed and appreciated.

It's to do with recognizing how things such as rhythm, pitch, timbre and tone work together. You can show this by composing, singing or playing an instrument, and by appreciating other people singing and playing instruments.

ACTIVITY

Alone: Put on any piece of music with a distinct rhythm. Choose a part of your body that moves freely. (It's probably best to do this activity in private.) Now move that part of your body in time to the music. You're using one part of your musical intelligence – the ability to keep time.

You may ask, 'How do I know if I'm in time?' Good question. Maybe someone who is known for their sense of rhythm (and who won't embarrass you) could watch you and tell you how you're doing. Or maybe you think, 'Oh, I've never had a sense of rhythm – I blame my music teacher.'

However well, or not, you thought you were keeping time, you were using part of your musical/rhythmic intelligence, the areas of your brain that are wired for rhythm and movement.

With your learners: If you get the chance to sit back and observe your learners while music is playing, notice who is tapping their hands, feet or fingers in time to the music.

For a unique take on the musical intelligence, have a look at www.voicetraining.co.uk.

Book shop

I wander down to the book shop: there are floors crammed with books of all shapes, sizes and subjects – from Beckham's biography to Tolkien's tales, with poems, recipes, advice, humour, facts and opinion in-between. The shop is full of language, lovingly carved to entertain, enlighten, express, and to influence. This is the heart of the **verbal/linguistic** intelligence – the ability to use language.

Verbal/linguistic intelligence

Your potential to think in words and to understand how language is used effectively.

It's to do with the skills of reading, writing, speaking and listening and using them to describe, inform and persuade. You see this intelligence in lawyers and politicians when they are trying to influence or convince others. It was used quite a lot to launch the National Literacy and Numeracy strategies.

I browse the shelves of the education section, looking for a copy of my first book. (*How to Create and Develop a Thinking Classroom*, LDA, if you're interested.)

I'm rather surprised to be an author. From junior schooldays I still remember the weekly force-feed of spellings and the utter frustration of handwriting practice. However, I also remember being pretty good at talking myself and my friends out of trouble with the bigger boys. I've avoided many fights by my careful use of language – I still do when I'm running some INSET days. But being able to blag your way to safety was never as valuable as having neat handwriting and ten out of ten for 'ight' words. Typing away here at my laptop, spelling and grammar checks on, I know which skill is more valuable to me now.

ACTIVITY

Alone: Imagine that you are sitting in a radio studio, at a table, with a microphone in front of you. One minute from now you will be live, broadcasting on air. But this isn't local or even national radio. When the 'on-air' sign glows, the whole world will be listening. Your words will go around the globe, translated and re-broadcast and transcribed and passed on by word of mouth, until everyone alive has heard you. Your words will reach every corner of every country. But there's a catch: you can broadcast only ten words in your own language. You have one minute to think up your ten words. Start the clock now – what would those ten words be?

_____

_____

_____

_____

With your learners: Bring the focus onto specific learning objectives: summarizing a story; describing a mathematical operation; evaluating a D&T product; giving an opinion; critiquing a piece of art; summarizing the day's learning.

The words can be written or spoken and the time limit/word count set to meet the linguistic abilities of your learners. Over time, you can reduce the time given and the number of words allowed.

The salon

It's been quite a busy morning, so time for a bit of pampering at the hair salon. I used to visit a barber's, but since I've been working with learners in the hair and beauty industry, I have a 'design and cut' instead of a 'number 3 up the back and sides; short and spiky on top please'.

My hairdresser is very clever. Like us all, she has each intelligence to varying levels, but she excels when she deals with people. Happy clients come back to her, and her business thrives if she manages her team effectively. She understands how people tick. She knows from their expression, posture, words and intonation just how they are feeling, and she can predict how they will react. She's skilled at relationships: discussing a client's needs; managing her team of stylists; or planning the growth of her business. She uses her **interpersonal** intelligence.

Interpersonal intelligence

Your potential to think about other people and to understand the relationships you have with them.

It's to do with your knowledge of how people behave and your use of this to get along with them effectively.

After my shampoo and Indian head massage, I ask my stylist for a number 3 up the back and sides; short and spiky on top, but she insists on discussing my needs properly first. Then, as she snips away effortlessly at my hair, we talk about the salon's new intake of trainees. Some are low on self-esteem, so the salon has decided to use MI to address this. Within a few days of joining, each trainee has their MI profile pinned to the wall. Every time they pass it, they see a public affirmation of how they are clever.

I buy some gooey stuff to smudge through my hair every morning, and say goodbye, scratching at snipped hairs under my collar, and very happy with my haircut.

ACTIVITY

Alone: Open your personal phone book at random and dial the first number you see. If there's no answer, try a different random number. When you do speak to someone, talk with them for about ten minutes, then bring the conversation to a close without being rude. You could say that you're doing an experiment and need to go away and make some notes. Now think about the person you have just spoken with. How were they feeling? Do you think your conversation altered the way they were feeling in any way? How did they react at different points during the conversation, and why? If you know the person well enough, you could perhaps phone back and find out what they thought.

This can be quite a difficult activity, both to do and 'assess', because a lot of information that your interpersonal intelligence makes use of is either missing or distorted – there is no body language or facial expression and speech is altered by the phone.

With your learners: Best not to encourage them to repeat the above activity. Instead, to sample their interpersonal intelligences, you could ask them to observe other people – during breaks, in different classes, at lunchtime – and think about how these people might be feeling. Tell them to look for body posture, facial expression, speed and type of movement; and to listen for not only the words but how they are spoken.

This observation activity could also be run during lessons. How do people act and move when they are learning effectively? How can you tell if someone is feeling good about their learning?

Computer store

My computer is 'on holiday'. Over the last few months it has slowed down little by little, like an enthusiastic jogger coming to the end of the London marathon. I left it with the professionals for a boost, and I'm off now to collect it.

I got my first PC in 1980 – an Acorn Atom with 2Kb of memory, which was just enough to run a game called *Sheepdog*. In *Sheepdog*, your cursor was the dog; many white dots were the sheep. The aim was to herd the sheep into a pen (three connected lines). It was tricky because the sheep were programmed to avoid the dog, but stick together.

Before long I tired of this game and learned to program the computer myself. Eventually, I discovered how to reprogram *Sheepdog* to make the sheep gather around the sheepdog rather than run away. The dog simply walked into the pen and the game was over.

Today I use a computer with 30 million times more memory than the one I had in 1980 – though the box itself is half the size – and I have immediate access to well over a billion pages of information via the internet. I can chat and share photographs by email and I can buy most of my Christmas presents online.

This phenomenal, continuing and sometimes overwhelming growth in communications technology is due to the **logical/mathematical** intelligence. Physicists, mathematicians and technologists work tirelessly to explore and exploit the boundaries of science. Through hypothesis, experiment and logical reasoning they have speeded up, shrunk and vastly enriched the potential of technology.

Logical/mathematical intelligence

Your potential to think logically and to reason about the connections between objects, actions and ideas.

It's to do with thinking in straight lines – if–then thinking; knowing about cause and effect. This intelligence gives you the skills to create strategies, to explore, examine and work things out and score well in IQ tests.

The strategic thinking of the business world applies these technological discoveries for our benefit. The cogs and wheels of commerce have turned the scientists' findings and inventions into our tools and entertainment. And at the store I'm pleased to find that the technicians have used their considerable logical/mathematical skills to give my computer a new lease of life.

ACTIVITY

Alone: Answer this question: If the weight of a sheep is 40kg plus half its own weight, how much does it weigh?

The right answer is not necessarily important – wrestling with the question is. By having a go you engage parts of your brain that look after logical reasoning. Don't spend too long on the problem though – you may begin to use other bits of your brain involved with feeling frustrated. In the best tradition of puzzles like this, the answer appears upside down at the bottom of the page.

That challenge may have raised painful memories of algebra lessons. Or you may have found it a doddle! And it is unfortunate that intelligence is sometimes linked only to this sort of question – one that is easy to do if you know how to do this sort of question!

With your learners: An easy way to challenge them to think logically is by turning learning objectives into logical arguments – by using if–then. For example, the objective:

'To be able to multiply two three-digit numbers' becomes:

'If you can multiply two three-digit numbers, then...' and learners finish it off:

'...you can multiply two two-digit numbers' or

'...you can speed up addition' or

'...you can solve problems'.

Answer: 80kg. We don't know the sheep's weight, so call it X. 40kg plus half of X equals X, or 40 + X ÷ 2 = X. Each side of the = sign is the same. Double each side (sides still equal each other) – 80 + X = 2X. Remove X from each side – 80 – X = X. So X = 80kg, the weight of the sheep, is 80kg. Now have a large glass of fortified wine and a good rest.

DIY store

I'm now at the DIY warehouse, a vast building stocked with row upon row of tools and materials for the amateur builder or would-be landscape gardener. I used to take ages to find what I came in for, but with a bit of thought I've discovered that it's quite easy to get around.

The store is organized by product type – roughly one aisle for each. Along each aisle, products are usually arranged by brand. These categories then divide again into sizes, colours or styles. For example, a five-litre can of value white matt emulsion is classified and placed like this:

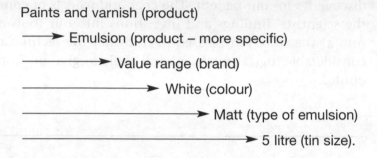

Paints and varnish (product)
Emulsion (product – more specific)
Value range (brand)
White (colour)
Matt (type of emulsion)
5 litre (tin size).

Every item, from a 10mm panel-pin to a new kitchen, has its place in the hierarchy of DIY. And this is the essence of the **naturalist** intelligence – the classification, organization and recognition of things in the environment and discerning fine differences between similar things.

Naturalist intelligence

Your potential to think about and understand the natural world.

It's to do with your ability to recognize and classify plants and animals and other aspects of your environment. It's about appreciating nature – weather systems, lakes, rivers, farms – and buildings, cars and people. And there's more to it than going camping every weekend.

These skills and talents have their origin in our cave-dwelling days – at a time when we needed to know if a certain berry would poison or nourish us; whether a certain animal would eat us or we could eat it. And these skills are still alive and active in our modern urban environment.

I pick up some 10mm panel-pins and wander into the garden centre. As before, the plants and garden materials are arranged in a strict order. The tags on the plants display their common and Latin names and often the family – their place in the plant kingdom. I'm not much of a gardener, but I have kept several house plants alive for at least a couple of months. I choose a *Dionaea muscipula* (Venus fly trap) to replace the *Chlorophytum comosum* 'Vittatum' (spider plant) that died last week.

ACTIVITY

Alone: Look around you. You may be outside, in your home or at school. Look at the objects in your environment. Note them down and classify them. If you are in the garden, you could arrange items into living and non-living (include yourself), then reduce each group by size, shape, colour and so on.

With your learners: Carry out a similar task in the classroom. At the start of the year this activity can particularly help with organization and management of resources – all learners get to contribute to classifying the work area in their own way, helping them to locate and then tidy away materials and tools. For example, to find A5 lined paper:

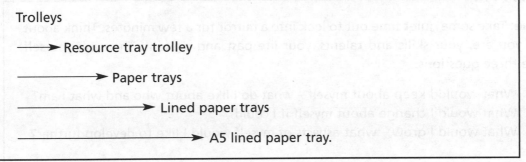

Trolleys

⟶ Resource tray trolley

⟶ Paper trays

⟶ Lined paper trays

⟶ A5 lined paper tray.

Online auction site

It's time for a bite to eat, and I go back into town to an internet café. It has baguettes and broadband, so I buy a BLT and settle down in front of a PC to check my email. (Three genuine messages and 17 from someone called 'Viagra'.) After I've replied (to the genuine ones), I log on to see if anyone's auctioning 10mm panel-pins.

Online auction sites usually look after themselves very well. They don't need much patrolling because their users self-regulate. If you provide goods as you've described and deliver promptly, or pay on time, you receive positive feedback, which builds your reputation as a trusted buyer or seller. Conversely, if you post late, send faulty goods or don't pay, you receive negative feedback and a damaged name.

It's fascinating. The range and quantity of things for sale are awesome. When I looked this morning, there were 402 toothbrushes – most of them new. One 'genuine' used-by-Beckham hotel toothbrush had a reserve price of £200!

Selling and buying online like this needs the skills of the **intrapersonal** intelligence: the self-motivation to buy and sell on the internet; the knack of building your online reputation; the ability to handle the knocks when your beloved tea set doesn't sell, or to bounce back from unfair feedback (or a non-payer); the ability to make decisions and choices for yourself; and the self-control to work alone and patiently at your laptop – possibly long into the night – to put a final bid on that celebrity-owned toothbrush you've always dreamed of.

Intrapersonal intelligence

Your potential to think about yourself and to reflect on your thoughts, feelings and actions.

It's to do with how well you know yourself and what you do with the knowledge. This intelligence gives you the skills to set your goals; to work towards them realistically; and to consider the 'you' part of your relationships with others.

ACTIVITY

Alone: Take some quiet time out to look into a mirror for a few minutes. Think about who you are, your skills and talents, your life past and present. Then ask yourself these three questions:

1. What would I keep about myself – what do I like about who and what I am?
2. What would I change about myself if I could?
3. What would I grow – what aspects of myself would I like to develop further?

With your learners: Ask them to do the same, perhaps bringing it to bear specifically on learning:

1. What learning skills would you like to keep?
2. What learning skills would you like to change?
3. What learning skills would you like to develop?

Time for coffee

I've arranged to meet a friend in the café. He's a headteacher from a local school and a very deep thinker. But that doesn't get in the way of his being a very practical and effective school manager.

I've known this friend for over ten years and I can't ever recall making 'small talk' with him. Instantly we're away; discussing the books we're reading at the moment, films we've watched recently, people we've seen since we last met. We talk about ideas and issues and consider how this relates to our philosophies of life. We argue, discuss and debate. He's an atheist-humanist with Buddhist sympathies. I have a Christian background and I'm interested in concepts common to all religions and belief systems. So, we have a lot to talk about.

Conversations in coffee shops, cafés and bars are when we tend to put the world to rights and explore our place in the universe; where our **existential** intelligence kicks in.

Existential intelligence

Your potential to think philosophically and to understand life, the universe and everything.

It's to do with your ability to deal with questions about life, death and human existence. This intelligence gives you the skills to contemplate your place in the universe and to explore and express the beliefs by which you live your life.

Recently, I've been learning to meditate. I've read books, listened to gurus, set time aside to practise and kept a diary of my progress. In that time I think I've managed one second of semi-enlightenment. Meditation is a slippery pursuit – the more I think about it and attempt it, the more it eludes me. I seem to have the most success when I stop trying.

Meditation is one way to express your existential intelligence. At the moment, existential is known as a 'half intelligence', but colleagues in the States tell me that Howard Gardner is looking for further evidence to equate it with the others.

ACTIVITY

Alone: Find a place to be alone. Sit in a comfortable position. Keep your eyes open. Become aware of your breathing – there's no need to alter it; just notice it. Now choose an object or point in front of you and look at it. Keep your attention on it. Thoughts will spring up, noises may be heard, your body may ache. Acknowledge the thoughts, feelings, sounds and aches, then let them pass, like clouds drifting (or speeding) in front of the Sun. Bring your attention back to your object or point. As thoughts and feelings come, continue to acknowledge them, let them pass, and then focus your attention once more. Do this for as long as you want – a minute, ten minutes, twenty.

With your learners: I've always thought that young children are more in tune with existential ideas than us 'baggage-laden' adults. They are full of questions about the universe, and they are not afraid to ask them: 'Where did I come from?', 'What colour is God?', 'Why do people die?'. If you are working with younger children, ask them, 'What's the biggest question you can ask me?'. Set some time aside for answering.

The existential intelligence is used naturally in RE, but can be called on in other subjects. Short meditations with music can prepare pupils for learning and the question 'Why?' can help. Take an idea linked to any learning objective and ask, 'Why?'. Then ask why to the answer and keep going. Like a curious child, you'll eventually get to a deep question about life, the universe and everything – to which the answer will be '42', 'Because', or 'There goes the bell'.

Case study

Resource : Meditation in school
Teacher : Rebecca Nelson
Location : Beeston County Primary School, Beeston

Rebecca has studied the use of meditation in the classroom. She sent questionnaires to 70 schools and of the 37 who replied, 9 said they were using meditation. These were some of the reported positive effects on the children:

'Many are more relaxed and receptive.'
'They do go to play more calmly.'
'More calm and receptive to learning.'
'Definitely much calmer after the (meditation) session.'

Rebecca's search for findings to build on didn't bear much fruit, and she concludes that more research is needed. She also recommends that teachers take the right training if they plan to use relaxation programmes in class. Visit www.discovery-project.com, for example.

The gym

After a tough day shopping, I could either: relax in front of the TV or go to the Pilates class my wife has recommended.

My local fitness centre has a gym, relaxation rooms and a range of classes. These classes have moved on since the aerobics of the 1980s and 1990s. We now have body-balancing and Pilates and if you've tried either, you'll know how difficult some of the moves can be. Pilates needs a great deal of concentration, body awareness, flexibility and strength. This is my first session.

After some 'easy' starters I'm now focusing my way into one of those 'breathe out, stretch and hold (for ages)' positions. I'm trying to think about which parts of my body should be doing what. I'm aware of muscles and joints and body shape and I'm thinking about how to move in to and out of this challenging position. I'm using the brain areas responsible for body control – part of the **bodily/kinesthetic** intelligence.

Bodily/kinesthetic intelligence

Your potential to think in movements and to use your body.

It's to do with your ability to control your body and to control things with it. This means sport, dance, art, craft and brain surgery.

An hour later, stretched and sweating, I head for the changing rooms. I take my shower things out of my locker and put my glasses in (I can just make out the top letter on the optician's chart without them). When I return, dried and dressed, I remember my £1 deposit in the locker. It's stuck and peeping out from its slot. I pinch it tight and pull. I use my nails. I attempt to dig it out with my car keys. I try bashing it; pinching and pulling it with both hands; spinning it in the slot; rattling it; wobbling it; and finally, swearing at it. It remains stuck. At this point I become aware of a very large and muscled man near by. Even without my glasses I see he is not happy. I have been trying to liberate his £1. I smile and get my specs from the neighbouring locker.

My attempts to steal £1 from Arnold Schwarzenegger used other features of the bodily-kinesthetic intelligence – the skills of manipulating objects. I also needed my interpersonal intelligence to manage this situation. Saying, 'finders keepers' to this man would have been MI suicide!

ACTIVITY

Alone: This activity gives some indication of your bodily-kinesthetic skills and is best done behind closed doors. Or at least in the staffroom. You can also use it to great effect during an Ofsted lesson observation. Stand on one leg with your eyes closed and both arms outstretched. How long can you stay like this? The record at the time of writing is held by a headteacher in Portsmouth who stayed balanced for two minutes and ten seconds.

With your learners: With appropriate health and safety considerations, ask them to try the above.

Department store

This leisure day has been a light-hearted tour of the intelligences. As you'll see, each intelligence comes with a wealth of serious, supporting scientific evidence. But first, we need to go to a department store.

If a single high street shop represents a single set of skills, then the department store stands for them all; if a single shop links to a specific set of brain areas, then the department store symbolizes the whole brain. In a collection of departments, under one roof, you can buy furniture, sports equipment, music, computers, hair and beauty products, books, coffee and flowers – and many other items – each representing one or more intelligence. The department store can bring MI into the real world by combining the intelligences as they are in our everyday experiences.

 Multiple intelligences

Your potential to think, act, solve problems and create valuable things in eight and a half (nine) different, equally valuable ways.

It's to do with your whole range of skills and talents, driven by the activity of different sets of brain regions. It's your ability or opportunity to think about how you are clever rather than how clever you are.

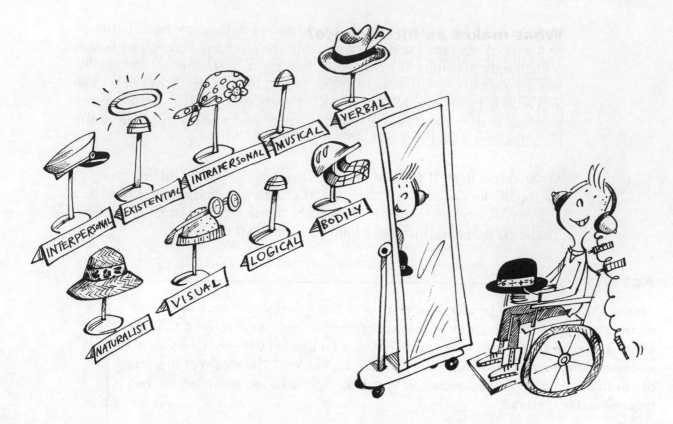

Intelligences rarely work on their own. Most tasks in life need a special combination of skills, just as different products represent more than one intelligence. Does a book about Vivaldi activate musical or linguistic skills? Is a Pilates video visual or bodily? Which intelligences do we use when we are digging the garden on a rainy day? Naturalist? Kinesthetic? Intrapersonal? Visual?

Introducing MI into the classroom

Classroom display is a powerful way to introduce MI to your learners. Choose a theme then think up nine examples on the theme – one to represent each intelligence. Make this into an interactive display in your classroom or a corridor. I decided on shops as a theme for my introduction; you could choose hats, celebrities, products, phrases or any other theme suiting the age and maturity of your learners. For example:

Age group	Themes
Special needs nursery	Photographs of children doing activities; modelling language and actions
Pre-school	Toys; everyday objects; photographs of activities; nursery rhymes
5–7	School equipment and resources; parents' jobs; jobs/skills of cartoon characters
7–11	Hats (see illustration above); shoes; school subjects; hobbies; famous people
11–16	Subject-specific displays: geography – places; maths – patterns; music – genres, composers and performers; English – characters from novels, lines from poems
Post 16	Vocational themes – hair and beauty tools; engineering tools; media equipment
Adult	Key life events; careers

What makes an intelligence?

The Lilliput Antique Doll and Toy Museum on the Isle of Wight is, not surprisingly, full of antique dolls and toys. If you can draw yourself away from the amazing collections of Lego and Meccano, Barbie, Cindy, teddy bears, Scalextric cars and Hornby trains, there's a corner at the back of the building with something even more interesting in it.

There is a display of soft toys from the middle of the 20th century. Look closer and you'll see that one of the cuddly figures is in fact Adolf Hitler. That doesn't feel right – a soft toy version of one of history's most evil men – but it's there, and it raises a valuable point about MI: soft wadding can be used to make cuddly animals or 'cuddly' despots; the stuffing doesn't distinguish between filling Winnie the Pooh and Adolf Hitler – the stuffing is neutral.

The same goes for the intelligences – they are not good or evil in themselves; they can be used for peacemaking or warmongering; for creating or destroying; for good or evil; for helping or hurting.

Thankfully, we get a chance to learn a sense of right and wrong – morality – which helps us to choose how we use our gifts. Hitler was a very intelligent man, especially skilled with words. But his warped morality applied this linguistic talent (and others) to the destruction of freedom. Gandhi was also a highly intelligent man, and used his linguistic intelligence (and others) in the pursuit of liberty.

A moral intelligence has been proposed, but Howard Gardner rejects this idea. In *Intelligence Reframed*, he writes, 'Morality is a statement about personality, individuality, will, character – and, in the happiest cases, about the highest realization of human nature.'

If morality is about how we use our intelligences, but isn't one itself, what makes 'an intelligence'? The existential intelligence is only a 'half' not because its skills are any less valuable than the full eight – but because there is not yet enough proof to confirm its existence.

Howard Gardner assesses a 'candidate' intelligence like existential or moral against eight criteria, and when enough evidence has been collected to meet the criteria, the intelligence is approved and added to the list. Only one intelligence has so far been added to the original seven drawn up in 1983 – naturalist in 1996.

Rejected candidates are usually cocktails of the other intelligences. Shopping, for example, can call on the skills of decision making, motivation, financial management, visualization and planning – all linked to various existing intelligences. Nonetheless, let's take some examples to see how a 'shopping intelligence' measures up against the recognized verbal/linguistic intelligence.

To meet the eight criteria, Gardner says that an intelligence must have:

1. 'an identifiable core operation or set of operations…'
   which refers to the various skills that are produced by the intelligence

Linguistic	Shopping
• Using words to persuade or inform • Understanding grammar • Knowing word meanings • Identifying different sounds	• Identifying a need • Finding a product to meet the need • Choosing a product • Buying a product

2. 'a distinctive developmental history, along with a definable set of 'end-state' performances…'
   which means that the skills grow (through learning) eventually to match the needs of certain careers

Linguistic	Shopping
From early babbling to a language degree and onwards, word skills develop along a well-defined road – 'Da da' comes before 'Drink please'; Nick Butterworth before Nick Hornby. Careers relying in part on linguistic skills include: • Politician • Lawyer • Teacher • Writer • Negotiator • Translator.	Is there a difference between buying a penny chew in the corner shop and financing a mortgage on your first house? If so, then maybe shopping does have a developmental history. As for 'end states' or careers, my wife tells me there are *professional* shoppers, and an internet supermarket order needs a 'shopper' in the store to fill the trolley before a van brings it to your door. You can also become a 'secret shopper' where you are paid to shop, and must provide detailed feedback on your experience.

3. 'an evolutionary history and evolutionary plausibility…'
   which means that the skills have grown and changed as humankind has evolved

Linguistic	Shopping
Linguists tell us how languages emerge and evolve around the world. They explore how spoken and written forms of communication change over time. For example, they tell us that English, Bengali, Polish, Welsh, Irish Gaelic and many others derive from a prehistoric language called Proto-Indo-European. They also track the appearance of writing from its roots in pictograms and symbols.	Most of us would struggle to hand over two chickens and a sack of carrots in exchange for a Robbie Williams CD. So you could say shopping has evolved.

4. 'support from experimental psychological tasks…'
   which means psychologists have tests for it

Linguistic	Shopping
It's harder to do a crossword while listening to a song than it is while listening to music with no words. The crossword and the lyrics compete for the language areas of your brain. Music is handled by different regions, so does not stretch your linguistic resources. Psychologists have many tests like this to show that the intelligences are separate.	Is shopping performance affected by other intelligences? Is it as easy to shop while playing table tennis as it is when chatting to a friend? Can you carry out two transactions at once without your performance suffering? (This must be a PhD waiting to happen…)

5. 'support from psychometric findings…' which means there are tests for it	
Linguistic	**Shopping**
Yes.	I don't think so…

6. 'susceptibility to encoding in a symbol system…' which means that the intelligence can be represented in some way	
Linguistic	**Shopping**
The symbols of language are the marks we make – letters combining into words building into sentences, paragraphs and texts.	I don't know of symbols that specifically represent shopping skills, but there are many symbols associated with it – brand logos; 'Enter your PIN'; £; $; %; &; ½; €.

7. 'examples of idiots, savants, prodigies and other exceptional individuals…' which means there are special needs and gifted people with respect to the intelligence	
Linguistic	**Shopping**
Have you ever been taken in 100 per cent by an inspirational speaker, or laughed till it hurt at the jokes of a stand-up comic? Have you ever heard the bodily genius Wayne Rooney give an interview? The use of language exists across a vast spectrum of competence.	Consider the groups 'most men' and 'most women' for evidence of the broad spectrum of shopping ability.

8. 'potential isolation by brain damage…' which means that the skills are lost if key parts of the brain are damaged	
Linguistic	**Shopping**
A stroke is devastating. A blood clot damages areas in the brain causing loss of function – usually speech, movement or vision. If areas on the left side of the brain are harmed, speech can become slurred or lost altogether.	Are there specific brain regions which provide our shopping abilities? I honestly don't know and I think by now you will have realized that shopping falls short of the eight criteria!

How to be brainy

As discussed earlier, if we value each part of our physical brain equally then the skills and talents produced by each part of that brain must be equally valuable. Isn't a six in cricket as valuable as a poem; a sculpture as worthy as a physics experiment? This is one of the best arguments you can use to defend MI and promote its benefits. Here are the specifics:

It is accepted by most neuroscientists that different areas of the brain look after different functions. But it's not the case that one single brain area drives one function. Networks and combinations of areas look after broad collections of activity. These collections aren't fixed – the brain is flexible and dynamic; it evolves and self-organizes in response to its surroundings.

With new brain-scanning techniques and shrewd experiments, scientists are beginning to tell just which networks drive which actions. The list below is illustrative only and incomplete (and I'd be interested to hear from neuroscientists who can develop it for me).

1. Brain areas associated with aspects of the verbal/linguistic intelligence – specifically reading and speaking

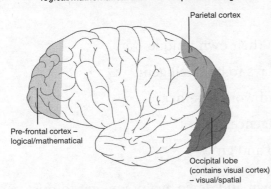

2. Brain areas associated with aspects of the bodily/kinesthetic intelligence

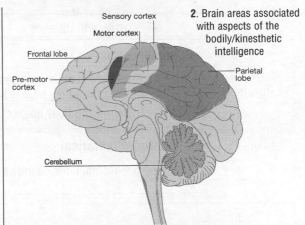

3. Brain areas associated with aspects of the logical/mathematical and visual/spatial intelligences

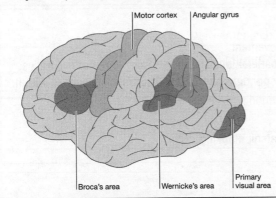

4. Brain areas associated with aspects of the interpersonal and intrapersonal intelligences

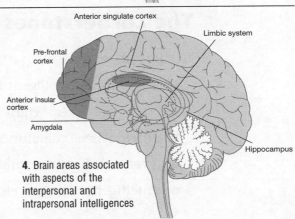

Verbal/linguistic

- Located mainly in the left hemisphere, around and above the ear.
- Broca's area co-ordinates the mechanics of speech.
- Wernicke's area makes spoken language comprehensible.
- Angular gyrus is concerned with meaning.

Musical

- The right auditory cortex springs to life at the sound of music.
- The limbic system registers the emotional tone of music.

Existential

- The 'God Spot' found in the temporal lobes fires up during prayer and meditation.

Interpersonal and intrapersonal

- The amygdala is the brain's alarm system. It sends information to the conscious brain and is a clearing house for emotions.
- Part of the cortex generates a social 'Have a nice day' smile.
- The unconscious brain generates the genuine, or 'Duchenne' smile.
- The anterior insular cortex registers disgust.
- The anterior singulate cortex fixes your attention, motivation and persistence.
- The pre-frontal cortex controls impulses and plans ahead.

Visual/spatial

- The right hippocampus and parietal cortex help you find your way around a space.
- Different parts of the visual cortex look after various aspects of vision:

  V1 – general scanning   V4 – colour
  V2 – stereo vision   V5 – motion.
  V3 – depth and distance

Bodily/kinesthetic

- The pre-motor cortex executes movement.
- At the junction of the frontal and parietal lobes lie the sensory and motor cortices. Each area of the body has a corresponding part of these cortices associated with it.

Logical/mathematical

- The pre-frontal cortex handles strategic thinking skills.

The cornerstones of MI

To summarize, remember:

- Everyone is intelligent in their own unique way.

- There are at least eight ways to be intelligent.

- Intelligences combine and work together.

- Everyone has each intelligence.

- Intelligences can develop and grow.

If you distil MI theory right down and down again, you get to this:

Everyone is clever.

That's the heart of it, and if you believe it deep in your bones, MI theory and practice will come to you naturally.

MI researchers and educational practitioners from around the world gather regularly to share their learning and experiences. The AERA – MISIG (American Educational Research Association – Multiple Intelligences Special Interest Group) meets each year in a different American city. In 2002, after an address from Howard Gardner, Larry Cuban, an urban high school teacher, made the point that multiple intelligences theory has had:

- the highest impact on schoolteachers' belief and talk about children's intelligence

- moderate to high impact on the formal curriculum and instructional methods

- little impact on mainstream teaching practice.

Teachers believe in MI, talk about it and adjust their plans, but they don't change their teaching. Section 2 will show you how this can be achieved.

Using MI

Preparing to use MI

'People, you see, are so very different.'

Fyodor Dostoevsky

Having come this far, the last thing I want you to think is that MI is 'another thing to do', 'a new initiative' or 'one more strategy likely to tip my work-life balance the wrong way'. MI is a different way of viewing your work and a boost to what you do well already – not an addition.

This section of the book looks at the practical nitty-gritty of using MI in the classroom and showing your learners how clever they are. It includes:

- seven different ways of infusing MI into your teaching

- practical suggestions and case studies to plan your own development of an 'intelligent classroom'

- extracts from a teacher's diary as she begins to use MI with her pupils and creates an intelligent classroom.

This section describes how I and other educators have used MI in practice: what we did and what happened as a result. The ideas help to deliver curriculum content and support school improvement, but you need to decide if and how you will implement them. Use the following questions to guide your thinking as you read and to consider if an idea will help you and your learners to succeed:

- Will it work for me?

- Does it feel right?

- Will it help me to teach more effectively?

- Will it help my learners learn more effectively?

- How can I apply the idea? Does it need to be adapted? Is that easily done?

- Do I have the time to do it?
- What are the benefits for me, my learners, my school?
- What could get in the way of doing it?
- What will I see and hear in my classroom if I am successful?

The MI spiral

Some educational experiences can be represented by a straight line, progressing steadily from one to the next.

But with a straight line, outcomes can't influence what happens next.

This could be put right with a circle: outcomes provide information to make the next experience better.

But a circle doesn't go anywhere except round and round. Another representation might combine a line and a circle like this:

Progress is implied by movement to the right and the results of one experience lead into the next. However, the final loop can be a very long way from the first one.

A spiral puts this right and this is why I have chosen a spiral to symbolize the infusion of MI into teaching and learning. It shows feedback by going round and round, and progress by growing outwards. Each part is fairly close to every other one, even though a great distance has been travelled. Learning is connected and evolving.

On a spiral, each stage of teaching and learning grows out of the ones before, yet remains connected to them. You can move at your own speed – maybe stopping now and again or even reversing to take another look.

Creative solutions

In March 2002, Chris Woodhead, then Chief Inspector of Schools, published an article in the *Daily Mail* entitled 'Learnacy? This is Lunacy'. He used his column inches to launch an attack on 'learnacy' (the concept that learning itself can be learned) of which multiple intelligences is a part. He said, 'Think about it for a moment. Seven intelligences, five different approaches, 30 children in the class. That is more than 1,000 permutations to hold in your head.'

The quote references Michael Barber (then the Campaign for Learning's key adviser) who proposed five approaches to a lesson, each mapping on to one intelligence. This is duplication and means that we're only looking at five times 30 possibilities – but 150 levels of differentiation is probably a little too much to ask even of the most accomplished teacher.

Mr Woodhead was spot on with his observation. He brought his logical and linguistic strengths to a challenging educational innovation. Obviously it would be very difficult and time-consuming to give each student the curriculum matched to their unique intelligences.

But logical strengths can at times become limitations. There are many straightforward ways of using MI without having to prepare each lesson in hundreds of ways. If you want to find them, there are always creative solutions. Where teachers succeed with MI, we find them offering a range of MI-inspired activities over a period of time – maybe a visual/spatial bias one week, and a verbal/linguistic one the next; maybe a choice of two activities, or an opportunity to be valued for every skill – not just handwriting.

An approach like this keeps learning manageable while respecting individual abilities. Over time, as teacher and students get to know each other, approaches can be refined and activities matched more accurately.

The rest of this section offers simple, inventive solutions to the rewarding challenge of using MI. Working out from the centre of the MI spiral, the development of MI can grow naturally through the following stages.

- Stage 1: How to understand MI
- Stage 2: How to speak MI language
- Stage 3: How to build MI profiles
- Stage 4: How to create an MI environment
- Stage 5: How to teach and learn with MI

This sequence isn't restrictive. As long as you have a basic understanding of the theory, you can pick any area to explore on its own, or in combination with others.

Stage 1: How to understand MI

The more you use MI the more you understand it, but it's a good idea to know the basics before you begin. Section 1 of this book goes some way to explaining what MI is all about. The following text includes suggestions for sharing this learning with your colleagues.

In his book, *Becoming a Multiple Intelligences School* (published by ASCD), Tom Hoerr (who kindly put some words at the front of this one – and do visit him at New City School in St Louis if you can get international study money) suggests we get to grips with MI theory as a whole staff:

'At one of our weekly faculty meetings in spring 1988 I told the staff about a fascinating book I had read, Frames of Mind *by Howard Gardner. I was particularly excited because I thought it might have implications for our work with students... I proposed that we all read the book and take turns presenting chapters to the group... "But since we believe in team teaching," one of the teachers responded, "why don't we team-teach each chapter, working in groups of two?" Another teacher said, "And if the idea is that children possess strengths in different intelligences and we are going to want to think about using them in our teaching, shouldn't we try to teach with the different intelligences?"'*

Over the following months, Tom and his staff slowly, carefully and creatively brought MI theory to life. Since then, they haven't looked back and Tom now welcomes over 800 international visitors each year to New City School – to see how they 'do' MI. He recently opened his school's new MI Library – a wonderfully rich environment where both the architecture and resources reflect all intelligences. (See page 120 for notes from my visit to the school.)

Tom's collaborative approach can be used for any new theory that a school wants to put into practice – everyone is involved, everyone has a part to play, everyone has ownership of the theory and the practice. Inspired by Tom's ideas, below is a plan for preparing and holding a series of four meetings to help school managers who want their staff to develop an understanding of MI.

Getting to grips with MI theory in five easy steps

Step 1: Preparation

- Establish a rationale for using MI to enrich teaching and learning (the tricky bit).

- Make a personal commitment to using MI in school.

- Choose a suitable MI text, read it, then get a copy for each member of staff.

Step 2: Staff meeting 1 (1 hour)

- Explain the rationale and reasons for committing to MI.

- Present a brief summary of MI theory and practice.

- Distribute books and allocate sections or chapters to small groups.

- Give groups the next session and the remainder of this one to read their section and prepare an activity to teach to everyone else – the activity must reflect one or more of the intelligences.

Step 3: Staff meeting 2 (1 hour)

- Reading and activity preparation time.

Step 4: Staff meeting 3 (1–2 hours)

- Small groups teach their section of the book to the other groups, using an MI-inspired activity.

- After each activity, groups feed back their understanding to the whole group.

Step 5: Staff meeting 4 (1 hour)

- Develop MI-inspired action plans linked to new-found understanding and integrated with the school improvement plan.

In *Intelligence Reframed*, Howard Gardner suggests further activities for deepening an understanding of MI and using it well:

- Learn more about MI theory and practices.

- Form study groups.

- Visit institutions that are implementing MI ideas.

- Attend conferences that feature MI ideas.

- Join a network of schools (that are exploring and using MI ideas).

- Plan and launch activities, practices or programmes that grow out of immersion in the world of MI theory and approaches.

The diary of an MI teacher

Between September 2003 and June 2004, primary teacher Natalie Earl used MI theory to enrich her teaching. Extracts from some of her diary entries from this time are included at appropriate points in this section of the book – to bring to life the reality of infusing MI into a busy curriculum, itself sitting within a crowded educational world. Natalie and her class also kindly agreed to be recorded on video. This recording was possible thanks to a grant from Best Practice Research Scholarship (BRPS) and extracts can be viewed online at www.thinkingclassroom.co.uk.

Natalie works at Craneswater Junior School in Portsmouth. She qualified as a teacher in 2002, and in August 2003 offered to learn about multiple intelligences and see if and how it could help her and her pupils in the classroom. Natalie is open to new ideas, but she is also down to earth in her expectations. She is a real teacher in a real school and recorded her thoughts throughout the year as she attempted to create an intelligent classroom. Here is her first diary entry.

Day 1   7.30 pm

1 2 3 4 5 6 7 8 9 10 11 12 13 14 15 16 17 18 19 20 21 22 23 24 25 26 27 28 29 30 31

It's only been five days into the new term and already I'm thinking of what I will be doing in the half-term holiday!! The video team were in this morning. I was feeling a little nervous as I wasn't sure what to expect. Filming took place most of the morning with the children and myself. The children were very excited about being on camera, which is more than I can say for myself! During the afternoon I was bombarded with mountains of new information and terminology. Bit scary all these new intelligences. How am I ever going to learn them all?!

MI glasses

As your understanding of MI grows, you'll begin to think differently. If you are open to MI and let it flow into your consciousness it can alter the way you view people and the world.

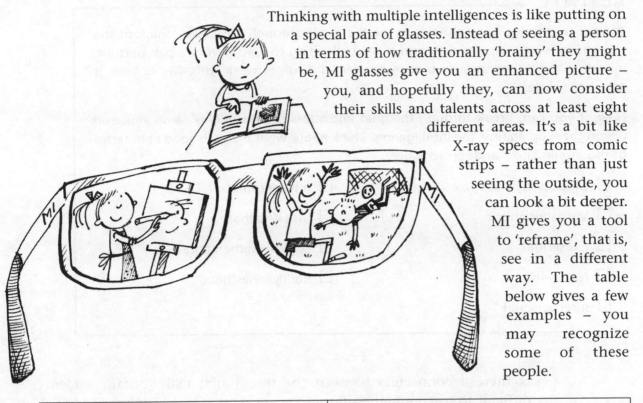

Thinking with multiple intelligences is like putting on a special pair of glasses. Instead of seeing a person in terms of how traditionally 'brainy' they might be, MI glasses give you an enhanced picture – you, and hopefully they, can now consider their skills and talents across at least eight different areas. It's a bit like X-ray specs from comic strips – rather than just seeing the outside, you can look a bit deeper. MI gives you a tool to 'reframe', that is, see in a different way. The table below gives a few examples – you may recognize some of these people.

Traditional view	View through MI glasses
A six-year-old girl who struggles with handwriting and reading, loves drawing and football and is popular with her classmates	A six-year-old girl who has interpersonal, visual and kinesthetic strengths that need to be applied in developing her linguistic skills
An 11-year-old boy with an IQ of 145 who feels isolated from and different from his peers	An 11-year-old boy with highly developed visual, logical and linguistic skills who may benefit from bringing these skills to bear in developing his interpersonal intelligence
A primary schoolteacher who uses music and art extensively in his teaching and has difficulty producing lesson plans in the detail required by the school	A teacher who uses his musical and visual intelligences to deliver the curriculum and who needs to develop his logical skills – possibly by applying the structural aspects of music or by planning his lessons as mind maps
A secondary school science teacher who excels in her scientific understanding and enthusiasm for the subject and who has difficulty forming relationships with students and colleagues	A secondary school science teacher with logical and naturalist gifts who could be supported in using these strengths to analyse and then improve her professional relationships
A parent who believes she is 'thick' because she didn't get maths O level and who has a knack of organizing fellow parents to support school fayres and other fundraising events	A parent with underdeveloped mathematical abilities who has a highly effective set of interpersonal skills

MI glasses help you to see what people are good at, and to visualize how they can improve. It shifts the focus from weaknesses by keeping the view balanced and inclusive.

ACTIVITY

Alone: To develop your abilities to see the world through MI glasses, think of the student (or students) who you find most challenging to teach. Write a pen portrait, including the things they do that make them difficult to work with. (Try to keep it reasonably brief!)

Now, if you can, break through the grief and stress these students cause you, and weigh them up against the intelligences. Think about what they are good at in terms of the intelligences and record it here:

☐ Musical/rhythmic   ☐ Intrapersonal

☐ Verbal/linguistic   ☐ Visual/spatial

☐ Existential   ☐ Logical/mathematical

☐ Naturalist   ☐ Bodily/kinesthetic

☐ Interpersonal

Is there a connection between the things that make certain students difficult to teach and the things they are good at? Liz Flaherty, SENCO at Cove School in Farnborough believes there may be.

Case study

Resource: Links between MI and 'disruptive' behaviours
Teacher: Liz Flaherty, assistant headteacher/SENCO
Location: Cove Secondary School, Farnborough

Liz uses MI theory to think about disruptive behaviour in class. She believes that each of the intelligences, and combinations of them, can be the cause of different 'problem' behaviours. She and her special needs team are always asking themselves what drives unacceptable behaviour. For example, when Darren taps and hums, is it a deliberate strategy to annoy the teacher, or an unused musical/rhythmic intelligence spilling over?

Liz says, 'Teachers need to be aware that these children are not being deliberately difficult or non-compliant. Effective differentiation would take these behaviours into account and capitalize on them. The curriculum is currently based on a model that presumes all children are, or need to be, linguistically or mathematically intelligent, but so many more students would be enabled to succeed if we could acknowledge, make provision for and encourage their individual styles of learning.'

Below is the table of 'disruptive' behaviours that Liz Flaherty has identified during her research. She links the behaviours to the different intelligences then considers how each behaviour/intelligence can be harnessed in learning: what activities make use of the intelligence that is otherwise going to waste?

Intelligence	Manifestation as 'disruptive' behaviour
Verbal/linguistic	• Checks repeatedly what s/he has been asked to do with teacher/peers • Chats as s/he completes a task • Has difficulty in maintaining 'exam conditions'
Logical/mathematical	• Asks why • Seeks clarifications such as: how much to write how many questions there are what the time is how much time is left
Musical/rhythmic	• Hums quietly under breath • Taps out rhythms on desk • Uses personal stereo mp3 player
Visual/spatial	• Needs to sit in 'his'/'her' seat • Likes personal area not to be obstructed • Behaves worse if in a strange room
Bodily/kinesthetic	• Finds it hard to sit still • Plays with equipment • Taps desk • Clicks pen • Leaves seat at any opportunity • Touches other pupils • Swings on chair • Fidgets
Interpersonal	• Likes to know what is going on in other people's lives • Chats about social life • Easily distracted by others • Likes to be the centre of attention
Intrapersonal	• Keeps head down • Reluctant to participate in class • Thinks things through for him/herself • Prefers to work alone • Does not seek out the company of peers
Naturalist	• Finds it hard to be in an enclosed room • Always looking out of the window • Likes to be close to the door

Day 4

10.45 PM

| 1 | 2 | 3 | 4 | 5 | 6 | 7 | 8 | 9 | 10 | 11 | 12 | 13 | 14 | 15 | 16 | 17 | 18 | 19 | 20 | 21 | 22 | 23 | 24 | 25 | 26 | 27 | 28 | 29 | 30 | 31 |

Visual, existential, musical, logical... What's that one about working together? Oh yes interpersonal; intrapersonal; writing, speaking and listening, that's linguistic, zzzzzz, getting tired now. There's one more. Ummmm... Naturalist. Excellent. Now how am I going to teach the children all these new terms? I'll worry about that tomorrow. ZZzzzz...

Stage 2: How to speak MI language

Two Year 4 boys come running into class after lunch.

FIRST BOY: Miss, he swore at me!

SECOND BOY: I didn't, honest!

FIRST BOY: You did, you said the f word!

SECOND BOY: I didn't miss, honest.

FIRST BOY: You did. You said I was fick.

We've seen how MI can change the way you think. It's a small step from there to adapting the things you say. Here are some examples of how MI language can enhance existing teacher talk:

'In PE today, our challenge is to improve our ball skills; so we're going to need our BK (bodily/kinesthetic) intelligence.'

'Why do we need to use our logical and visual intelligences in numeracy today?'

'Great! That's an effective sentence; good use of your linguistic intelligence.'

'Your challenge is to create a map of our local area. Which intelligences will you need to do this?'

'Look everyone, Liam's done well here because of his naturalist intelligence.'

If you use 'MI speak' in front of your learners, then they will use it too, especially as you travel through more and more stages of infusion, giving learners more exposure to the vocabulary of MI.

When I used language like this with a Year 4 class, most of the children adapted their own vocabulary without effort or complaint. Over the year, I noted four distinct stages of language use. This was exciting because the same things had happened the previous year, and in the same order, with a Year 3 class:

The development of MI language

Stage 1: The excuse

A couple of months after introducing MI, a child will use MI as an excuse:

ME: Kamal, please stand still outside Mr Maynard's office.

KAMAL: I can't because I'm BK.

ME: If you're BK then you should be able to control your body.

Stage 2: The parent's excuse

Four months in, parents use MI as an excuse:

MR NASH: He's linguistic you know, so he's going to talk in class.

This stage is encouraging because it indicates that the children have spoken to their parents about MI being used in school.

Stage 3: Spontaneous use

After six months, children use MI language without prompting:

ME: So why do you want to be a hairdresser and a runner, Bethan?

BETHAN: Well I reckon I could use my BK and inter [-personal intelligences].

Stage 4: Creative use

At eight months, some children begin to work out the intelligence profiles of their relatives and pets:

CHARLIE (in the middle of a science lesson, during which he has obviously been thinking about something other than the topic): Mr Fleetham, I reckon I know the intelligences of all my family and my baby brother too.

Charlie hadn't answered any questions or spoken in class until he volunteered that information, which was followed by:

CHARLIE: My cat's BK, visual and inter.

ME: How did you work that out?

CHARLIE: Because he catches birds and plays around with them.

A caveat to my time with Charlie was his admission towards the end of the year that he had successfully taught this same cat a series of Brain Gym® moves. Unfortunately I never had the opportunity to validate his claim.

It took a while to convince some learners that they were clever. The language and culture of multiple intelligences was confusing and threatening to them. Their identity, security and safety net seemed to come from a sense of not being clever. They had (very cleverly in fact) constructed a belief that 'acting stupid' made life easier and helped them to avoid hard work. 'I'm thick,' was mumbled openly and regularly by two children who were very cautious about this chance to be clever. By the end of the year, the message did reach them: 'OK, OK, I'll use my BK then, if you really want me to.'

And it was very encouraging to overhear an uncharacteristically kind nickname that this class had for their teacher: 'Intelligence man'.

Day 6

5.00 PM

1 2 3 4 5 6 7 8 9 10 11 12 13 14 15 16 17 18 19 20 21 22 23 24 25 26 27 28 29 30 31

An interesting day today. Getting to grips with the terminology now. Also starting to introduce MI vocabulary in the classroom. Still thinking about how the children are going to learn all this new stuff! Starting to think about how I can use this whole new concept in my teaching. Got some ideas floating around in my head already...

Your MI thoughts and MI language are one and the same. The strength of connection between what you think and what you say is very strong and illustrated well by the concept of political correctness: by being told what is acceptable/unacceptable to say you are automatically being told what is acceptable/unacceptable to think. Certainly, in some cases, rethinking and rewording are needed – especially if an individual or group are being disrespected or devalued. But to have real impact by what we say, first we need to alter what we think:

If your learners understand MI, think MI and begin to use its language, then over time their self-belief can shift. This was brought home to me very powerfully a few years ago with a Year 3 class. Using a short questionnaire at the beginning and end of the year, I discovered this inspiring and rewarding set of figures:

	Number of children who believe that...		
	'I'm clever'	'I'm not sure'	'I'm not clever'
September	13	15	2
The following July	28	2	0

The following activity rounds off our look at the first few stages of MI infusion – understanding, thinking and language.

ACTIVITY

Alone and **with your learners**: Have a go at the MI song over the page. It should help you all to remember the intelligences. It can go to the tune of 'Twinkle Twinkle Little Star' and has accompanying actions. The tune can be changed to suit the age of your learners.

Musical and linguistic

Conduct. Hands talk into ear.

Existential; naturalist

Hold chin and frown thoughtfully. Look to the horizon.

Inter-; intrapersonal

Both arms out. Arms across chest.

Visual; mathematical

Hands make binoculars. Hands out and count.

Or is it bodily...

Front crawl.

Which ones are right for me?

Both hands point to self.

Stage 3: How to build MI profiles

By now, you'll have a good grasp of MI theory and how it can enrich thinking and language. So, it's natural to ask, 'How am *I* clever and how are *my students* clever?' By compiling a profile to answer these questions you'll discover two things:

1. the activities that you are best at providing for your learners (based on your MI strengths)

2. the activities that your learners are most likely to engage with (based on their MI strengths).

NB: These two may not necessarily be the same.

There are several ways to build up a multiple intelligences profile, described in the following pages. You can pick one or more from this list. Most of them will already be part of your day-to-day work – all they'll need is an 'MI tweak'.

● Using questionnaires

● Observing behaviour

● Talking with parents

● Talking with learners

● Using performance data

● Using work samples

Before we look at the tweaks, a warning about questionnaires and profiling in general. Do you ever have a go at those multiple-choice questionnaires when browsing through magazines? When you add up your score, you'll probably get a number that tells you what sort of person/lover/ gardener/driver/dieter you are. If you get a 'good' score, you may feel better about yourself; if you get a 'bad' one, you either start worrying (about your self/partner/garden/driving/diet...) or go back and change your answers. Sometimes, there are recommendations based on your score, along the lines of:

0–25: Slow down and remember not to diet while driving, making love or digging up vegetables.

26–35: You need more broccoli in your life.

It can be tempting to apply the same process with MI questionnaires, but that's dangerous. MI is all about discovering and developing, over time, a range of talents within each learner. A questionnaire gives your first glimpse, but can turn discovery and development into labelling and limitation if it's the only profiling done.

Questionnaires cannot ask every possible question related to MI and may not give an accurate first impression of a learner, and questionnaires, particularly if self-completed, could appeal more to people with strong verbal and intrapersonal skills. Profiles also change over time as learners grow and experience new things. So it makes sense to build on questionnaires by using other ways of profiling. Even when other methods are used, we must still avoid *constraining* learners to their strengths.

If, for example, Max's MI questionnaire reveals that he has strong bodily and interpersonal intelligences then we should value and use these skills. But Max shouldn't be restricted to them. He may well need a boost to his linguistic intelligence – necessary for exam and future life success. His language skills can be improved by using what he's best at: interpersonal – paired writing, paired reading; bodily/kinesthetic – role play, charades.

An MI questionnaire is the opening credits to a dynamic and evolving movie telling the unique story of a learner's skills, talents, potential and achievements. And it's a movie that never ends – you never get to that final definitive profile – whatever combination of methods you use – because people keep changing and growing.

This is why you should avoid labelling (and potentially limiting) with any form of MI assessment. You don't want the movie to end just after the first reel. Remember:

● Build profiles by using more than an MI questionnaire.

● An MI profile is an ongoing process, not a product.

With that in mind, we'll now look at the different profiling methods. Then, the table on page 76 shows you how all of them can be integrated during a school year.

Using questionnaires

Before children complete a questionnaire, you might like to tell them some or all of the following points:

- This is not a test and it won't be marked.

- There are no right or wrong answers.

- Everyone will choose different answers and that's OK because everyone is different.

- The results will tell you what you're good at and help you to learn.

- The results will help your teacher to make your lessons better for you.

- It'll give you a chance to let people know what you're best at and what you like doing.

- Answer for yourself. Don't put down answers you think your teacher wants to see.

- Be honest

There are lots of questionnaires out there that can give you the first draft of a learner's MI profile. Two of the best can be completed online, the Birmingham Grid for Learning (BGfL) MI wheel and the MIDAS system.

The BGfL profile has been completed by over 50,000 people from all over the world. It's free to access at www.bgfl.org/multipleintelligences.

After answering 40 questions online, your MI wheel appears. It's a pie chart of eight coloured sectors representing the intelligences. Results can be stored online and accessed later using a password. MI wheels can also be printed out for reference and display. (See pages 78–85 for more on MI displays.)

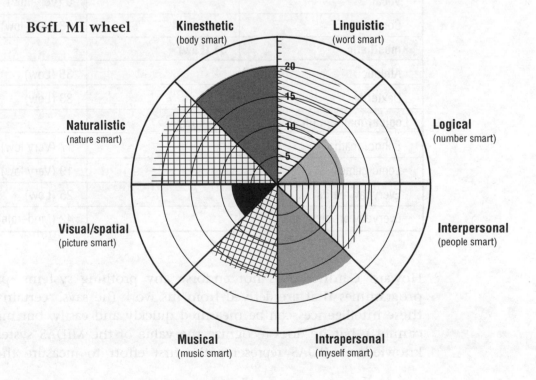

BGfL MI wheel

- **Kinesthetic** (body smart)
- **Linguistic** (word smart)
- **Naturalistic** (nature smart)
- **Logical** (number smart)
- **Visual/spatial** (picture smart)
- **Interpersonal** (people smart)
- **Musical** (music smart)
- **Intrapersonal** (myself smart)

MIDAS, which stands for Multiple Intelligences Developmental Assessment Scales, is an online inventory of 70–120 questions, dependent on age. Five versions are available, from pre-school to adult, at www.miresearch.org/onlineassessment.php.

Developed by Dr Branton Shearer, lecturer at Kent State University in Ohio, MIDAS is considered to be the Rolls-Royce of MI profiling and has over 15 years of research and validation behind it. It's not free, but it's well worth the investment because it goes much deeper than a basic profile. It's the only MI questionnaire to break down each intelligence into its component parts. The musical intelligence, for instance, is made up of four subscales: appreciation, composition, vocal and instrumental. The subscales are then averaged to give you an overall musical score, but the value of each subscale is also shown because the averaging process can hide a high-scoring subscale. For example, a very high level of 'musical appreciation' would not be recognized if the other three scales were very low and pulled down the average.

In this extract from a MIDAS profile, if the details from the subcategories were not included and taken into account, the moderate musical score of 47 could easily mask the very high Instrument score (100). Likewise, the low logical/mathematical score (25) is partly made up from a moderate problem-solving score (42).

Scale	Score	Category
Musical	**47 (Moderate)**	
Appreciation		60 (High)
Instrument		100 (Very high)
Vocal		0 (Very low)
Composer		13 (Very low)
Kinesthetic	**34 (Low)**	
Athletic		35 (Low)
Dexterity		33 (Low)
Logical/mathematical	**25 (Low)**	
School maths		17 (Very low)
Logic games		19 (Very low)
Everyday maths		25 (Low)
Everyday problem solving		42 (Moderate)

Howard Gardner does not endorse any profiling systems, products or programmes that are derived from his work (he says, 'certain aspects of these intelligences can be measured quickly and easily, but many others cannot'), but he does recognize the value of the MIDAS system: 'To my knowledge, MIDAS represents the first effort to measure the multiple intelligences that has been developed according to standard psychometric procedures. Branton Shearer is to be congratulated for the careful and cautious way in which he has created his instrument and offered guidance for its use and interpretation.'

Dr Shearer uses MIDAS as a starting point, but then puts further effort into guidance and interpretation. The first questions asked after the profile is completed are:

- Do the results feel right?

- Do they match what you already know about yourself?

- Would those who know you recognize you from your MIDAS profile?

In MIDAS profiling, it is OK to disagree with the results – what you and others know about you is just as valid to your 'total' profile as the numbers on the computer printout.

Day 7

6.40 PM

1 2 3 4 5 6 7 8 9 10 11 12 13 14 15 16 17 18 19 20 21 22 23 24 25 26 27 28 29 30 31

What a busy day today already and I still have to read another chapter of that MI book*! Handed out all the intelligence surveys today to the children and completed one myself. Wonder which will be my strongest intelligences...

* *Intelligence Reframed* by Howard Gardner

If you're unable to spend time online or pay for a profiling tool, a paper-based version – a simple set of questions that will get you going – is presented as a list on page 124 and a mind map on page 125. Each intelligence includes a question about 'getting into trouble at school', which will test out the idea presented on page 50 that misbehaviours in class may be related to untapped MI potential.

If your younger learners can't read the questionnaire, you may need to present the questions in a different way. The case study on the following page shows how the teachers at one infant school have developed resources to do just that.

Case study

Resource :   MI questionnaires for younger learners
Teachers :   Elspeth Simpson, and Sue Harris, headteacher
Location :   Pinewood Infant School, Farnborough

The school has 90 on roll and a resourced provision for language impairment. The school is wholly inclusive – children with language impairment (LI) are taught within mainstream classes, and withdrawn for specialist work and therapy. Classes are kept small.

Elspeth is SENCO and manager of resourced provision for LI. She has known about MI theory for some time and has always believed, 'everyone is good at something and it is our role as teachers to find out what that is.'

Elspeth says, 'MI has enabled me to talk to colleagues about their children in terms of what they can do rather than what they can't do. It has also clarified the mismatch between verbal ability and other intelligences. We have several children with autism spectrum disorders whose interpersonal skills may be weak but other intelligences are highly developed; this has enabled staff to emphasize the positive and not make assumptions about ability based on verbal skills. This also enables them to talk to parents about their children's achievements and expectations as well as their areas of needs.'

Finding out what pupils are good at is key to this approach. The school wanted a profiling method matched to the communication abilities of learners. Headteacher Sue Harris explains how they went about getting one:

'Initially our collective ideas of a profiling method were based on questions about how children felt when engaged in a particular activity. The children's answers would take the form of colouring a face depicting the emotion that best matched their feelings about that activity.

'I undertook a small-scale study and discovered that the children's responses were not as reliable as they could be. Despite our best intentions at simplifying the language, it was proving a barrier to all but the oldest or more able children.

'I carried out the study again, asking the questions verbally while showing photographs or objects relating to the activity. The responses were much more animated and children began to talk about what was happening in the picture or recalled a similar activity. The responses were generally more rounded and indicated a fuller understanding of what had been asked.'

Sue says that MI has had the following effects in school:

- *Conversations about children now focus on what they can do rather than what they can't and all staff are beginning to recognize children's strengths.*

- *Our understanding of 'intelligence' has moved beyond what can be measured.*

- *Planning is gradually evolving to reflect a range of activities for learning.*

- *Informal observations show that children are more engaged in their learning.*

- *Negatively – I think about all the children who passed through our classes before we were aware of MI!*

The resources mentioned in the case study are included on pages 126 and 127 for you to use and adapt with your learners.

The questions on the sheet 'MI through feelings' (page 126) cover a range of intelligences and all begin with 'How do you feel when…', with one of four responses – happy, neutral, sad, angry – to be coloured in. The repetition and focus on feelings can help young children who may not know if they are good at PE for example. That said, those of you who work with younger children will know all about their variable ability to judge their own performance and how it can be influenced by you and by peers.

The 'Visual MI questionnaire' template can be used for creating your own visual MI questionnaire. You'll need to take photographs around school to match the descriptions, or equivalent ones that represent the range of intelligences. Lay out large prints on the table for discussion, alongside the recording sheet (which could include thumbnail versions of the photographs).

Work one-to-one with pupils to discuss the series of photographs. Encourage the pupil to talk about the images through guiding questions such as:

- Which of these would you most like to do?
- Which are you best at?
- Which don't you enjoy?
- Which are you not very good at?
- Which do you want to get better at?

As you work with each child, use a highlighter pen to record preferences and therefore likely intelligence strengths on a personalized copy of the sheet. Recording is made easier if the photographs on the table are arranged in the same way as on the recording sheet.

Day 12

12.45 PM

1 2 3 4 5 6 7 8 9 10 11 12 13 14 15 16 17 18 19 20 21 22 23 24 25 26 27 28 29 30 31

Yippee!!! The children were so inquisitive about their profiles. There were so many questions and so much excitement. 'What's linguistic, Miss Earl?' 'What're your strongest intelligences?' 'Does Visual mean I'm good with my eyes?' It was really difficult not to say too much as I was planning to deliver a lesson on MI language for the children on Monday. It was great to see them looking at each other's profiles and realizing that they all had different intelligences. It's all starting to come together!

Observing behaviour

I went recently to an end-of-term concert: 250 children from local infant, junior and secondary schools assembled in a theatre, packed with proud parents and tired teachers. I was up in the circle, looking down on the stage and the performers waiting in the stalls.

The first act was a secondary school orchestra, and while it kicked off with the theme from *The Great Escape* my eyes were drawn to the younger members of the audience. As the tune progressed, some of them sat absolutely still, some tapped their feet; others bounced their legs, and a few were either conducting or moving their whole body from side to side. A small number were alternately standing and sitting in time to the beat. From the circle above, it looked like a huge frying pan full of sizzling, jumping vegetables.

Thankfully, the teachers didn't intervene to stop any of this behaviour. Each child's response to the music was a key to part of their multiple intelligences profile – the rhythmical and appreciative aspects of the musical intelligence.

Every day, there are thousands of actions and interactions in a classroom: learners talking to each other, moving around, looking, choosing, arguing, listening, laughing and sulking; and teachers instructing, sighing, intervening, guiding, frowning, smiling, and drinking coffee. Some actions pass unnoticed; others stand out. The ones that stand out while you're wearing your MI glasses (see page 49) are the ones to be interested in now. They'll give you further information about emerging MI profiles.

Observations can be targeted in several ways and it's advisable to keep them simple. Watching for signs of all intelligences, in each learner, in every lesson is not recommended. You could focus on:

- a single child
- a group
- a specific subject linked to an intelligence
- evidence of one intelligence
- a specific activity.

The resource on page 128 is pupil-centred. It lists things you might see children doing to indicate specific intelligences, but the list is not complete, so you can add your own observations.

I'm not particularly successful when it comes to strict record keeping. I prefer a more spontaneous approach than religious form-filling and rigorous filing of 30-plus observation sheets, because that's the way my brain is wired. A pad of sticky notes and a pen in the pocket is my preferred, but no less comprehensive method.

Whenever you spot MI-related behaviour, write it down on a sticky note (with the date and pupil's name) and then slap the note loudly, and perhaps with a theatrical flourish, onto the board. You may be invited to share with the class what you saw and why you valued it. However, do be sensitive to pupils' preferences with regard to public compliments and comments.

At the end of the day, peel the observation notes off the board and transfer them to a folder full of sheets of paper – one sheet for each of your pupils. By the end of the year, you should have a mosaic of MI sticky-note comments for each learner.

> 26/5 Callum
> Moving in seat in time to music while watching The Jungle Book DVD – Musical.

> 6/1 Hassan
> Upset when Jade 'accidentally' moved his maths book and pens out of the neat line he'd put them in – Logical? Naturalist?

> 16/2 Kyra
> Went over to a Year 1 boy who was crying and cheered him up – Interpersonal.

> 12/12 Billy
> Noticed him fidgeting more that normal while listening. Have given him quiet beanbag to occupy his hands – Kinesthetic? Is he worried about something? Call mum.

What you'll observe depends partly on how well each intelligence is represented in your classroom environment. Have you been able to provide opportunities for each intelligence to shine through? For example, lots of books, stories and talking will draw out linguistic behaviours; an absence of musical instruments, singing and CDs will reduce the musical ones. We'll look more at this in Stage 4: How to create an MI environment, on page 78.

The Spectrum classroom

Howard Gardner and colleagues thought about observation and environment back in the mid-1980s. It was around the time when he declined the advances of companies who wanted to offer MI profiling and testing. Instead of creating another battery of tests, his team took a different line – the Spectrum classroom.

They created a comfortable, resource-rich environment where children could naturally demonstrate their spectra of intelligences. The first 'Spectrum site' was for pre-school children and was well stocked with opportunities to trigger different intelligences – board games, art materials, musical instruments, areas for exercise, dance and building, specimens from nature and so on.

In *Intelligence Reframed*, Gardner notes, 'We assumed that children would find these materials inviting, that they would interact with them regularly, and that they would reveal to us, by the richness and sophistication of their interactions, their particular array of intelligences. Hence the title Spectrum.'

After several years of development, Spectrum was working as planned for children between four and seven years old. Children who visited the Spectrum classroom regularly, had their choices observed and then assembled into rough-and-ready MI profiles.

It had taken time to identify materials that would appeal to children of different ages, inclinations and social/cultural backgrounds. Gardner and his team also had to develop what they called 'bridging activities' – alternative ways for children to show their intelligences: 'for example, if a child didn't want to tell stories about a picture, we gave her props and encouraged her to build a diorama [a three-dimensional miniature or life-size scene in which figures, toy animals or other objects are arranged in a naturalistic setting against a painted background]. Using the diorama as a bridge, we then asked her to tell us what had happened to the people or animals in the diorama.'

For further information about the Spectrum Project, visit: http://pzweb.harvard.edu/Research/Spectrum.htm.

For a school, a dedicated Spectrum classroom would be an expensive luxury, but the Spectrum approach can be used in any learning environment. Anne Cassidy, a foundation stage teacher in Portsmouth, took on the idea and used it to profile her children then adapt her teaching.

Case study

Resource : Using MI in the foundation stage
Teacher : Anne Cassidy
Location : Paulsgrove Primary School, Portsmouth

Paulsgrove Primary serves an area of high deprivation. It has well over 600 pupils, aged between three and 11.

Children entered Reception with poor levels of function, despite having an excellent start in the school nursery. The classes contained, on average, 30 children, one teacher and one nursery nurse. With colleagues, Anne decided to assess Year R children for their MI strengths.

'The project was two fold; using foundation assessments from nursery, and observing children's learning choices during "free" time. We mapped the different elements from the foundation assessments onto the intelligences. We then set up a classroom rich in MI activities. We spent the next half-term observing specific (but different) children each day.

'Patterns of behaviour emerged as we focused on the children's first and second choice of activity during free time. We assumed these to be their strongest two intelligences. We then compared our observations to the nursery assessments and saw that 75 per cent of the children matched in one or both intelligences. It confirmed that kinesthetic learning was strong and linguistic poor.

'We then began to inspect our teaching plans and add activities to ensure MI coverage in any half-term. Phonics seemed an obvious place to start as we already offered a multisensory approach. Gradually we introduced MI into mental maths, self-directed learning sessions and themed work. We felt happier that we were addressing the needs of all our children, and we realized that our previous curriculum had offered little music, space to learn on one's own and movement to aid learning.'

Talking with parents

'Oh, she's always writing in her diary.'

'He's very popular you know, kids always calling round, he's always out with his friends.'

'Her dad can't spell to save his life, but he's dead brainy.'

'Yes, she loves singing and she's a majorette too on Thursdays.'

'He just won't do his reading for me!'

How often have you heard comments similar to these during parents' evening? If you listen very closely (with an MI ear trumpet, maybe), you'll gather some interesting news about children's MI profiles.

Tony Blair once said that being a father was more challenging than being Prime Minister. I'm not sure whether that tells us more about the Blair family or the state of the UK at the time, but those of us who are parents or carers will take his point.

All the pain, joy, frustration and reward of bringing up children makes parents and carers, whether they realize it or not, experts – experts in the children they look after. The time they spend with their children, in all forms of family relationship, gives them a vast store of knowledge. Most parents and carers can tell you instantly:

- what their children are like
- when they learned to do various things such as walk and talk

- what they enjoy doing
- what they are good at
- what they avoid doing
- what motivates them
- what demotivates them
- how they choose to spend their time
- what they dream of doing when they grow up.

This expert knowledge links directly to the child's MI profile and is a gold mine of information for the teacher.

So, how can we tap into this valuable deposit? Well, the system is already set up – the parents' evening. A typical first parents' evening is generally a fairly informal affair when parents and teacher get to size each other up. The focus is usually social and emotional rather that academic – parents need to know that their young one is happy, and teacher checks out what sort of support she can look forward to over the coming year. It's also a great opportunity to gather some MI information.

I once asked parents and carers to review the year their children had spent with me. They answered a short questionnaire, mainly about the impact of MI in the classroom. The results were very interesting. Out of 36 children, 27 had regularly (at least once a week, some daily) talked about school and MI with their parents. Children saying anything at all about school can seem a minor miracle.

I also discovered that six of the parents had started to use MI ideas in their own workplaces – from changed perceptions of work colleagues, to presenting management information in different ways. The benefits of bringing parents on-board may reach further than the classroom.

Here are three levels of gathering MI data from parents. The level you use information will depend on the MI approach in your school.

Level 1 (subtle): Use MI-inspired questions
During parents' evening, ask the usual 'settling in' and 'getting to know' questions, but add some that provide MI clues. The pro forma on page 129 gives an idea of how this might work. You might notice, for example, that the pupil:

- (linguistic) reads at home and practises spellings with mum
- (logical) enjoys playing chess and fantasy computer game with stepdad
- (musical) has a keyboard in his bedroom and tinkers with it most evenings; enjoys MTV
- (kinesthetic) goes swimming and to tennis every week, represents club in galas

- (intrapersonal) likes his own company – not many friends, seems happy with this

- (naturalist) looks after dog and two cats at home, great interest in TV nature programmes.

Level 2 (shared): Share the MI approach in advance

You can advise parents of MI and encourage their involvement by letter, sent out a few days prior to parents' meetings. It saves you explaining to each parent individually on the night and gives parents a chance to see their children with MI glasses. An example of the type of letter you could send out is provided below.

Preparing like this could work in your favour... or not. It could help parents give you a more accurate and considered picture of their children, or it could give them time and eight additional ways to overpraise or undersell them. Emphasize to parents that MI isn't about grades or comparisons with other children.

Dear Parent

Parents' evening

This year, we're developing our teaching to match children's different ways of learning. You'll appreciate that we're all good at different things – as are our students. We want to find out exactly where their strengths lie and use this to help them in the classroom.

We're using an idea called 'multiple intelligences'. It's a concept that is gaining popularity in many schools across the UK. It assumes that everyone is clever, but in different ways. If we can find out what those ways are, learning can be made easier and more effective.

In preparation for next week's parents' evening, please could you think about the following questions in relation to your child:

- What does s/he enjoy doing?
- What is s/he good at?
- What does s/he avoid doing?
- What is his/her favourite subject at school?
- What is his/her least favourite subject at school?
- What does s/he choose to do in spare time?
- What hobbies does s/he have?
- What would s/he like to be when grown up?

Your child's teacher will talk to you about this during your meeting. Your thoughts will be invaluable in helping us to plan more effective lessons.

Thank you.

Level 3 (full-on): Invite parents to an MI workshop

At this level, you'll want parents to be much more involved and knowledgeable. Through a hands-on workshop you can tell them about MI and have them create their own profiles. This will give them the confidence and vocabulary to describe their children to you in MI terms.

A workshop event like this can kick-start multiple intelligences in your school and will tap into parents' and carers' MI knowledge about their children. Hopefully, it will also pave the way for an ongoing MI dialogue between parent, teacher and child – a dialogue that will inform an evolving MI profile.

When planning and delivering an MI parents' workshop, be sensitive to your audience's starting point: remember that they could well have a traditional view of intelligence and a range of views on what school should be like. Here's a sample invitation.

Everyone is Clever – Parents' Workshop
Thursday 14 September 6.30 – 7.30 (coffee from 6.00)

Are you good with your hands?
Do you have a good imagination?
Did you get into trouble at school for talking too much?
Can you sing?
Do you find maths easy?

This year, we are developing our teaching to match students' different ways of learning. By using the concept of 'multiple intelligences' we aim to find out exactly where students' strengths lie and improve their learning.

You are invited to a workshop where you can discover your own multiple intelligences profile and help us support your child in this exciting new initiative. If you can put your hands on one of your old school reports, please bring it along!

We look forward to seeing you.

The workshop could take the following format:

- Welcome and thanks for coming
- Rationale behind choosing to use MI
- Parents fill out MI questionnaire (see page 130)
- Introduce each intelligence – refer to a famous person who could be seen to exemplify each one

- Share your old school reports and discuss how they match your strengths and weaknesses (be sensitive here)

- Parents share their school reports in small groups and discuss their MI profiles

- Explain how the school will be using MI

- Explain how parents can help in profiling their children

- Any questions.

As a spin on this, children could attend with their parents and fill out a children's questionnaire (page 124 or 125) when parents do the adult version (on page 130). There's a lot of scope here for family interaction – looking at how intelligences do or don't get passed down generations or through family environments.

Talking with learners

When your learners understand MI and know its vocabulary, they will be able to assess it themselves. With your help, they can reflect on the results of their MI questionnaire, their experiences in school, their activities outside school and even consider whether their parents' and carers' views of them are accurate.

Here, and on the next page, are the types of question that can get an MI conversation going, either between teacher and learner(s) or just between learners.

In school

- Which lessons do you most enjoy in school?

- Which subjects do you do well at?

- Do your favourite/best subjects match your strongest intelligences?

- Which lessons do you least enjoy in school?

- Which are your weakest subjects?

- Is there a link between these subjects and your weaker intelligences?

Out of school

- What do you do in your spare time?

- What clubs do you go to, which sports do you play?

- Is there a link here to your strongest intelligences?

Multiple intelligences

- Which intelligences are your strongest? How do you know this?
- What can you do that demonstrates this?
- What have you achieved that demonstrates this?
- Which intelligences are your weakest? How do you know this?
- What can't you do yet that demonstrates this?
- Do you need to strengthen your weaker intelligences?
- How can you strengthen your weaker intelligences?
- What would your friends say are your strongest/weakest intelligences?

Intelligence in general

- Who is the cleverest person in the class? How did you decide?
- Who is the cleverest teacher in school? How did you decide?
- Who is the cleverest person in the world? How did you decide?
- What is intelligence?
- Can someone get more intelligent? If so, how?
- Can someone get less intelligent? If so, how?
- Is everyone born with the same intelligence?

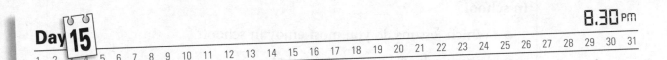

Day 15   8.30 pm

1 2 3 4 5 6 7 8 9 10 11 12 13 14 15 16 17 18 19 20 21 22 23 24 25 26 27 28 29 30 31

How clever everyone is! We had a circle time today and discussed our intelligences. I told the children that they were all clever but in different ways. This was a difficult concept for a few of them, perhaps due to low self-esteem. They couldn't accept that they were intelligent or clever. I'm hoping that this will rectify itself as the project unfolds. I was surprised how many of the children knew without looking at their profiles which were their strongest intelligences. What an amazing bunch of children.

The final two methods of MI profiling look at evidence produced by the learner – performance data and work samples.

Using performance data

Since I began using MI in my teaching and training, I've come across many people who feel let down by the education system. Sometimes, they have succeeded in life in spite of their exam results, rather than because of them. They don't have many 'A's to their name, but they've done well – like a hair salon manager who couldn't fill in the evaluation of my training session (because it was written feedback), but turned up in a Mercedes SL500 (that's a very expensive one) and was the admired boss of over 50 employees. Sadly, I also meet people who believe they have not been so successful. They failed their O levels/CSEs/GCSEs and never recovered. An MI perspective can sometimes undo this damage and release a person's long-hidden potential, but it is not always the case.

Exams and tests generally rely on a good memory, and parts of only one intelligence – reading and writing. If your talents lie elsewhere, you're going to need linguistic skills to get those talents valued publicly in your grades. For example, I work with many intelligent and successful hair stylists. They are successful because of their interpersonal, visual and kinesthetic intelligences. These skills are often already well developed when they start their training, but are not used to assess their learning. Instead they have to read multi-choice question papers and write long answers. Although 'performance data' is a part of the MI picture, it has usually been filtered through the linguistic intelligence.

It's also sad on the occasions when setting, streaming and grouping disadvantages mathematically strong children (usually boys) because of their below average linguistic skills: you can only be in the top maths group if you can read well. Believe me, I still come across situations like this in schools.

Whatever performance data you are using – SATs, foundation stage assessment, GCSE, NVQ and so on – consider:

- which intelligences the data maps on to
- that there won't necessarily be data for all intelligences (GCSE in emotional intelligence...?)
- that the data may not give a true picture of intelligences due to 'linguistic filtering'.

Using work samples

The different end products of learning illustrate the different intelligences. The things learners make, and how well they make them, tell you a great deal about their intelligences profile: a musical composition needs the musical/rhythmic intelligence; a clay figure requires bodily/kinesthetic, visual; and so on.

A great way to begin work sampling is to involve your learners straight away. Ask them to choose their favourite piece of work or an achievement of which they are proud. The list overleaf shows the sorts of things they could choose and the intelligences to which they are linked. (Of course, students' abilities to choose these products depends on their having had an opportunity to make them.)

These first choices should indicate areas of strength. Asking learners to identify the piece of work they think they could most improve will point to areas of weakness.

Favourite piece of work	Linked intelligence
Story, poem, reading record, book written or read, audio recording made, audio book listened to, notes from a debate	Verbal/linguistic
Graph, calculation, maths/science investigation results	Mathematical/logical
Composition, recording, dance set to music	Musical/rhythmic
Map, video, photograph, mind map, painting, sculpture	Visual/spatial
Model, sculpture, gym sequence, sports achievement	Bodily/kinesthetic
A product of teamwork	Interpersonal
A product made alone, diary	Intrapersonal
Tree diagram, Venn diagram, visit report/photographs	Naturalist

From this starting point, collect more samples of work and build portfolios of evidence. Seek out pieces from all intelligence areas and make it manageable by taking a year to do it: every five weeks, choose a different intelligence and collect one piece of work from each learner. Alternatively, select a couple of intelligences for the year and every five weeks collect pieces linked to them. The portfolios will then show a year's progression in these narrow areas, rather than snapshots over the full range. Or do both if you have the time.

Day 21 — 8.50 pm

Wow! Had a great idea today for teaching the children the different intelligences. Was watching 'Mr Benn' (yes I know I'm 29, but what a classic) and thought about how whenever he puts on a new costume he becomes that character. So, if each intelligence had a hat, then the children could use the hats to help them recognize each intelligence. Genius! Interpersonal could be an army hat - working as a team, visual could be those funny glasses with the big eyes. Naturalist could be a safari hat. Hmm... Will have to think about the rest.

7.50 PM

Day 26

1 2 3 4 5 6 7 8 9 10 11 12 13 14 15 16 17 18 19 20 21 22 23 24 25 26 27 28 29 30 31

What a fun day! This morning the children finally found out what all this new terminology meant. It worked really well with my hat idea combined with an MI story I used. The hats were given out to some of the children so they could remember the different intelligences. The children then had to decide which intelligence they thought was their strongest and go and stand with the relevant hat and child. It was very interesting to see where they all went and stood. The whole lesson helped the children to understand their profiles and what each intelligence meant. The jigsaw is nearly complete!

A class MI profile

At the start of the book we looked at personalized learning – remember the pineapple-squashing elephant? We considered the critics' view that genuine personalization for every learner makes teaching unmanageable.

It's fair to say that 30-plus profiled and personalized learners present a huge diversity of need to their teacher. To help address this valid concern we can generate and use a class MI profile. This is the average profile, generated from all the individual ones. It characterizes the teaching group as a whole, indicating the strongest and weakest intelligences. This in turn suggests the types of activity that the majority of the group will engage with.

For example, for the questionnaire on page 124, add up the total number of blocks coloured in by all your learners, for each intelligence, then divide each total by the number of learners. The result is a single profile describing the class as a whole.

Class profiles like this are invaluable when teaching with MI – see How to teach and learn with MI on page 87.

If you are serious about MI profiling, you will need to integrate it into your school assessment procedures. Perhaps you can adapt quite straightforwardly what you already do to take account of MI; perhaps you'll need to remove or add certain activities. Whatever you choose to do, these are professional decisions for you and your school to make.

The profiling methods suggested in the previous page can work alone or in combination. This table suggests how to use them all over one academic year:

Half term	MI profiling activity
1st	• Complete learner questionnaires • Interpret learner data • Hold parents' workshop leading to MI parents' evening meetings • Establish class MI profile • Take work sample (learner-led)
2nd	• Take logical and linguistic work samples • Observe learner behaviour, focusing on logical and linguistic
3rd	• Hold mid-year parents' meeting • Refine class MI profile • Take musical and visual work samples • Observe learner behaviour, focusing on musical and visual
4th	• Take interpersonal and intrapersonal work samples • Observe learner behaviour, focusing on interpersonal and intrapersonal
5th	• Take bodily and naturalist work samples • Observe learner behaviour, focusing on bodily and naturalist
6th	• Hold end-of-year parents' meeting • Repeat MI questionnaires, compare to originals • Assemble individual and class MI profiles to send up to next year group

Profiling in the future

Seven-year-old Ollie is starting school in a few weeks time, but he's at school today with his dad for a learning profile. They meet his mentor, Sally, and she leads them to a door marked 'Profiling Room'. Sally asks Ollie to take off his shoes then sends him through the door with the words, 'Have fun – go explore!'

Ollie enters a dark, hexagonal space. The lighting is low but colourful. On the floor are sensors. When he steps on them, the sound of a footstep, amplified, reverberates around the room. After a while the sound changes into other noises like choral voices, all triggered by the sensors hidden underfoot.

Two of the walls have huge interactive TV screens. A series of cameras project a silhouette of Ollie onto the screens. As he moves closer the image gets bigger. Other cameras enable the screens to react to touch.

As his confidence and curiosity grow, Ollie touches a screen and it changes colour. He touches it again and the pattern alters. He laughs at this and the sound is played back with an echo. He calls out, starts to sing, and his voice is played back. He runs to the moulded shapes on one wall, strokes them and hits them. Each one produces a sound and Ollie is surprised that the same shape doesn't always give out the same noise.

Ollie runs around the room touching, hitting, banging, singing and shouting, responding to the room as it responds to him. After a while, he sits down for a rest. He looks up at the black ceiling. Then he's off again, walking, running, stroking, hitting, singing and laughing.

After a few more minutes, Sally calls him out. Ollie appears at the doorway, smiling; puts on his shoes and grabs Dad's hand.

'How did he do?' asks Dad.

'I'll let you know next session,' Sally replies.

The room's computer already has a good idea of Ollie's MI profile. While he was interacting with his environment, sensors and cameras recorded his every move – where he went, for how long and how quickly he moved there. It picked up his words and his laughter. In the computer's memory there's now a file named 'Ollie' – a vast array of numbers describing the choices he made during five minutes in the room.

Later, Sally loads Ollie's data onto her own computer. Interpretation software indicates high potential in logical/mathematical intelligence because of Ollie's responses to the changing sequences of sound and light; notes a high bodily/kinesthetic strength from the quantity and quality of his movements; and flags up a moderate naturalist tendency from the overall curiosity he showed in the room.

Sally uses her experience as a facilitator of learning to make some recommendations for Ollie. These include activities to help him with literacy and numeracy, free-study topics and projects he is likely to enjoy, and after-school clubs that could develop his weaker intelligences. Even at this stage she proposes a range of careers he is likely to suit. She enters her ideas into Ollie's online portfolio so that his teachers can plan for his needs together with those of the other children in his new class.

This scenario is not as futuristic as it may seem. A profiling room like this already exists and has been trialled in the UK. MEDIATE is a collaborative research project involving universities in Portsmouth, Barcelona and Hilversum in the Netherlands. In 2004, researchers including Chris Creed from Portsmouth University built the room described above specifically for the use of autistic children. The computer files collected are currently being analysed to help psychologists better understand the needs of autistic children. With some further processing, the same files could be interpreted to reveal a realistic MI profile. Visit www.port.ac.uk/research/mediate for further information.

Stage 4: How to create an MI environment

You understand MI, can speak its language and think its thoughts. You have a pair of MI glasses and you know how to profile learners. So let's set about bringing this to life in the classroom. The ideas on the following pages aim to enrich your teaching and learning spaces.

Fleetham esteem board

(This is nothing to do with my self-esteem – I'm just the one who thought it up!) An esteem board like this is a great way to represent MI. Self-selected work indicates an MI preference, and intelligences charts represent the emerging profile. Three main advantages to having an esteem board in your classroom are:

1. You have a permanent and public affirmation that everyone in the class is clever.

2. You have an instant record of individual strengths. This can be used by teacher and learner alike to remind them of preferred approaches to learning.

3. You won't have to re-back your boards for the whole year – just keep replacing the work samples and updating the charts.

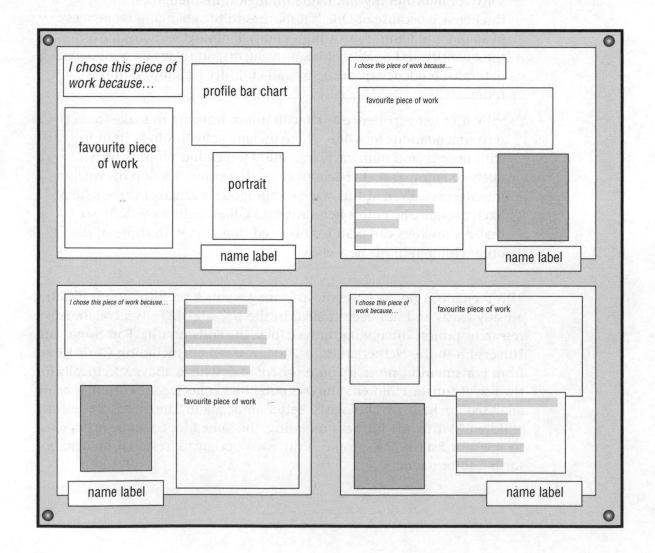

Making the board

If you have a teaching base (primary classroom/secondary tutor room) and have jurisdiction over its walls, set aside about 75 per cent of the available display space for your esteem boards.

1. Divide backed display boards into a grid – one 'cell' for each learner – including yourself and adults who teach with you. Use long thin strips of card, string or fabric to mark the divisions.

2. Ask your learners to personalize their spaces with name labels and drawn or photographic portraits.

3. After completing first draft MI profiles for each learner, display the results in their cell. One way to do this is using a horizontal bar chart. Each intelligence can have a bar up to nine blocks long. The longer the bar (the more blocks are coloured), the stronger the intelligence. Laminate the charts then use a whiteboard pen to mark blocks as follows:

   ■ Colour in one block for each intelligence (everyone shows some indication of each).

   ■ Colour in two further blocks for each of the two strongest intelligences (because everyone is intelligent different ways).

   ■ Colour in one extra block for each of the next two strongest.

This makes 14 blocks for each learner initially; these can be added to during the year.

Verbal								
Logical								
Musical								
Visual								
Bodily								
Interpersonal								
Intrapersonal								
Naturalist								

4. Ask your learners to choose a piece of work they are proud of, and display it in their cell. If this is not possible – a large piece of artwork or a new dance movement – help them to represent it with words, a drawing or a photograph. Ask them to caption their chosen piece by completing a phrase such as, 'I chose this piece of work to display because...'

Using the board

The board should be kept dynamic and alive:

- Every half-term, ask learners to take down their work and its caption, replacing it with another piece. Place the removed work and caption in an MI portfolio.

- At the end of term add more blocks to the charts to show how learners are developing their intelligences. Your ongoing profiling will indicate where new blocks should go.

- Attach sticky notes that record significant MI advances.

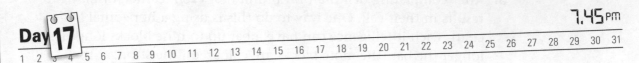

Day 17   7.45 PM

1 2 3 4 5 6 7 8 9 10 11 12 13 14 15 16 17 18 19 20 21 22 23 24 25 26 27 28 29 30 31

I am absolutely shattered. Didn't get home till six tonight. I received the results of the surveys. We worked solid for about three hours to get the display up so the children could look at their profiles. Seemed a lot of work but I know it won't have to be changed for the rest of the year. Each child had their own display space with their photo, name and profile. Each one was colour-coded to illustrate each child's strongest intelligence. Also I made a huge papier mâché head which was displayed in the middle, with each intelligence sprouting out from it. I was really pleased with the results.

Remember to keep checking on how things are going – and if something's just not working, change it or scrap it!

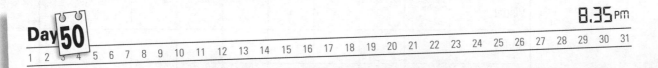

Day 50   8.35 PM

1 2 3 4 5 6 7 8 9 10 11 12 13 14 15 16 17 18 19 20 21 22 23 24 25 26 27 28 29 30 31

Those displays are just not working. It's been a term now and it's a nightmare to display the children's work in their individual spaces. Some children have decided what to put up, others haven't, some are writing up neat copies because they didn't want to put up their untidy version. Aaaargh! It's so frustrating. I have now decided to ditch that idea and will just have their profiles up with their photos and names on a separate display. The children's work can then be displayed on separate boards as normal. I think if the children had been older it could have worked.

LeFevre 'good at' board

This is named after Jonathon LeFevre, a deputy headteacher from Hampshire. Jonathon has asked me to say that his idea is not a classroom display of his O level and swimming certificates; rather, a LeFevre 'good at' board is a display area that encourages dynamic and evolving MI interactions. It should be put up in a place where everyone can see it during a lesson, and can be used in many ways:

- To introduce lessons, by fixing (with Velcro) a coloured star to each of the intelligences that will be needed, for example 'Working with others' and 'Words' before a shared reading activity.

- To build self-esteem and self-knowledge, by giving each learner two laminated name cards to stick on their strongest intelligences, photographing this, then repeating it later in the term.

- To build relationships, by allowing learners to nominate others who have succeeded with a certain intelligence.

- To develop formative assessment, by taking photographs of the board and thereby recording where learners have placed their name cards (repeating this during the year); by asking the learners which intelligences they have used; by asking learners which intelligence they want to improve and indicating this with name cards of a different colour.

- To deepen understanding of the intelligences, by adding photographs taken in class that illustrate the different areas, for example, learners doing PE in the 'Moving' section, learners painting in the 'Arty things' space.

If you try out this idea, you'll discover many more ways to use it.

MI resources

If you want to activate all of the intelligences in your teaching, you will need resources matched to each one. In a well-resourced classroom, you will probably have everything you need already. Things could be trickier in a science lab, or in a school with a limited budget, but provisions can still be made.

The table below lists two types of resource – active and passive – specific to the intelligences. Active resources are the tools, materials and furniture used to make things; passive resources are more part of the scenery. The lists are not intended to be exhaustive, but just one from each section will ensure full MI coverage.

Intelligence	Active resources	Passive resources
Verbal/linguistic	Books, audio recording and playback equipment, writing equipment, computer	Word wall, books, publishers' posters
Logical/mathematical	Calculators, computer, science equipment	Number tables/squares, reference formulae, flow charts
Musical	CD/cassette player, percussion instruments, manuscript paper, computer	Background music, concert poster, pop star posters, orchestra/instrument posters
Visual/spatial	Camcorder; digital still camera; art materials/media; OHP, acetates and pens; computer	Maps, 2D and 3D artwork, diagrams, coloured walls, travel posters
Bodily/kinesthetic	Construction kits/games, modelling clay, computer	Sport/dance posters, 3D artwork
Interpersonal	Flexible table and chair arrangements for: paired work, group-work, teamwork, presentations, debates	Multiple intelligences posters (see Further reading and resources), photographs showing different facial expressions, pictures of successful groups/teams
Intrapersonal	Flexible table and chair arrangements for: working alone, 'hiding away', thinking quietly	Multiple intelligences posters (see Further reading and resources), pictures of successful entrepreneurs
Naturalist	Magnifying glass, microscope, blank tree diagrams/taxonomies, pooter (for collecting minibeasts)	A window to the outside, ant/butterfly farm, aquarium, wildlife/nature posters, taxonomies/hierarchies
Existential	A space to think	Philosophical quotations, religious artefacts, pictures of philosophers and religious leaders

The final touches

You have now seen two types of interactive display boards and suggestions for classroom resources to create a multiple intelligences environment. Here are four quick and simple passive ideas (followed by a sample classroom floor plan on page 86 to bring it all together):

● Label areas of your classroom that link to one or more intelligences. For example, label the book corner and listening station: 'Linguistic area'; set aside individual seating, naming it 'Intrapersonal area'; an art area would be 'Kinesthetic and visual area'; and so on. This immediately raises the profile of MI without having to move or buy anything.

● Provide a series of objects on a theme to represent the intelligences.

● Display affirmations – first-person, present-tense, positive statements of intent that are read or said regularly. They fill your mind with optimistic thoughts, preventing the negative ones from getting a foothold. Here are three positive affirmations related to MI. Write them up as posters in your classroom and ask your learners to rehearse them daily – silently or out loud, depending on your and their level of comfort.

> I am intelligent.
>
> I am valuable.
>
> I succeed.
>
> I have unique skills and talents.
>
> I am becoming more intelligent.

● Quotations are highly distilled drops of wisdom. The examples on the following pages are organized to tie in with the multiple intelligences. They will give your learners something to think about in each area of talent. They could be displayed on walls, perhaps along with affirmation statements, or left out on work tables to inspire. Select those appropriate to your age group.

Verbal/linguistic

The poet doesn't invent. He listens.   Jean Cocteau, artist and film-maker

Poetry is plucking at the heartstrings, and making music with them.

Dennis Gabor, physicist

A poet's work is to name the unnameable, to point at frauds, to take sides, start arguments, shape the world, and stop it going to sleep.   Salman Rushdie, author

Naturalist

Nature does nothing uselessly.   Aristotle, philosopher

Human subtlety will never devise an invention more beautiful, more simple or more direct than does Nature, because in her inventions, nothing is lacking and nothing is superfluous.   Leonardo da Vinci, artist

Life has loveliness to sell, all beautiful and splendid things, blue waves whitened on a cliff, soaring fire that sways and sings, and children's faces looking up, holding wonder like a cup.   Sara Teasdale, poet

Interpersonal and intrapersonal

An insincere and evil friend is more to be feared than a wild beast; a wild beast may wound your body, but an evil friend will wound your mind.   Buddha

Remember, we all stumble, every one of us. That's why it's a comfort to go hand in hand.   Emily Kimbrough, author

Fear makes strangers of people who would be friends.   Shirley MacLaine, actress

He dares to be a fool, and that is the first step in the direction of wisdom.

James Gibbons Huneker, essayist and critic

Existential

Isn't it enough to see that a garden is beautiful without having to believe that there are fairies at the bottom of it too?   Douglas Adams, author

I don't believe in God but I'm very interested in her.   Arhur C. Clarke, author

Aim at Heaven and you will get Earth thrown in. Aim at Earth and you get neither.

C.S. Lewis, author

Musical

Music creates order out of chaos.   Sir Yehudi Menuhin, musician

You can never get silence anywhere nowadays, have you noticed?   Bryan Ferry, musician

Music was my refuge. I could crawl into the space between the notes and curl my back to loneliness.   Maya Angelou, poet and author

Music is the shorthand of emotion.   Leo Tolstoy, author

Visual/spatial

You don't take a photograph, you make it.   Ansel Adams, photographer

Artists can color the sky red because they know it's blue. Those of us who aren't artists must color things the way they really are or people might think we're stupid.
Jules Feiffer, cartoonist and author

An artist is a dreamer consenting to dream of the actual world.
George Santayana, philosopher and author

Logical/mathematical

Aerodynamically, the bumble bee shouldn't be able to fly, but the bumble bee doesn't know it so it goes on flying anyway.
Mary Kay Ash, businesswoman and entrepreneur

Your theory is crazy, but it's not crazy enough to be true.
Niels Bohr, mathematician and physicist

No amount of experimentation can ever prove me right; a single experiment can prove me wrong.   Albert Einstein, physicist

Bodily/kinesthetic

I've missed more than 9,000 shots in my career. I've lost almost 300 games. Twenty-six times I've been trusted to take the game-winning shot and missed. I've failed over and over and over again in my life. And that is why I succeed.
Michael Jordan, sportsman

Acting is a matter of giving away secrets.   Ellen Barkin, actress

It's good sportsmanship to not pick up lost golf balls while they are still rolling.
Mark Twain, author

Bringing it all together

As with all the ideas in this book, pick and choose what will work for you and your learners. This floor plan is an example of how some of the MI environment suggestions can be brought together in the primary classroom. Aspects of this approach can be adapted for use in specialist secondary classrooms. There is no particular reason for specific placement of the MI areas or resources, but the layout demonstrates that everything can be included.

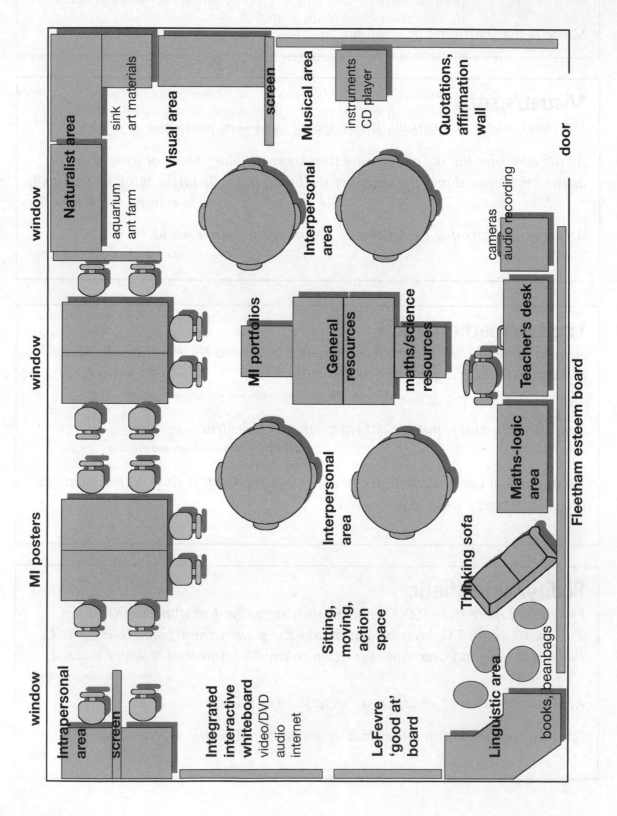

Stage 5: How to teach and learn with MI

There are two main ways to teach and learn using multiple intelligences:

1. Teaching and learning *to* the intelligences – teachers design personalized learning and assessment opportunities matched to learners' MI strengths.

2. Teaching and learning *through* the intelligences – learners do the personalizing by choosing from different MI activities/assessments to meet their curriculum goals.

It's a subtle, but important, difference.

In their book, *Multiple Intelligences in the Elementary Classroom: A Teacher's Toolkit* (published by Teachers College Press), Susan Baum, Julie Viens and Barbara Slatin have recorded dozens of ways that educators use MI for teaching and learning.

They have organized these approaches into five pathways. Four of the pathways explain the 'to' and 'through' of MI. (The fifth pathway looks at MI profiling and enriching teaching environments – which we've just covered.)

Following the 'to' pathways will develop and use specific intelligences and is teacher-driven. Following the 'through' pathways will develop a repertoire across a range of intelligences and is learner-driven.

Teaching and learning *to*...	
The 'building on strengths' pathway	The 'talent development' pathway
• support literacy development • 'bridge' student strengths to literacy learning	• design structured talent development opportunities • create opportunities to assess and nurture student talents
Teaching and learning *through*...	
The 'understanding' pathway	The 'authentic problems' pathway
• develop curricular options to enhance students' understanding • create diverse assessment options for students to demonstrate their understanding	• use real-world problems and expert roles • create authentic assessments of student learning

Later on, we'll look at these ideas in practice with several examples of MI teaching and learning (see pages 93–117). First, let's look at you, the teacher: you are how you teach!

An MI audit

When our diarist Natalie Earl first looked at one of her week's literacy plans, she discovered that the most frequent opportunities for learning were linguistic, interpersonal and visual ones. Natalie's three strongest intelligences are also linguistic, interpersonal and visual, so it's hardly surprising that her teaching reflects this.

Day 35

7.30 PM

1 2 3 4 5 6 7 8 9 10 11 12 13 14 15 16 17 18 19 20 21 22 23 24 25 26 27 28 29 30 31

It's a while now since the MI classroom has been established. I think it's been going pretty well so far. The children are a dab hand now at the language and use it all the time. They are even beginning to think of ways we can incorporate each intelligence into the lessons. This afternoon was spent auditing the literacy plan for next week to see which intelligences were being catered for. I was amazed by how many were actually used during the week. The only two that did not appear were musical and kinesthetic. I decided on activities that would incorporate them. I'm going to use music and actions to help create a bank of powerful adjectives and verbs to assist the children in their writing. I'm actually looking forward to seeing how this works out!

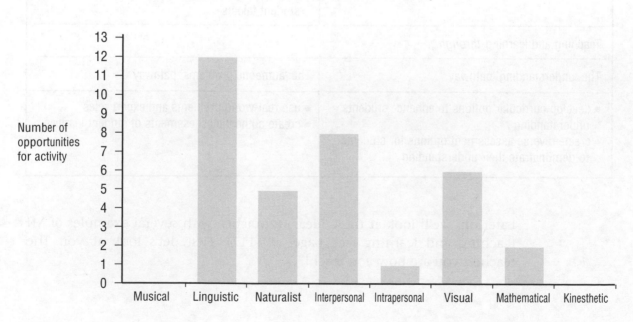

Natalie's MI activities in one week of literacy

Number of opportunities for activity

(vertical axis: 0 to 13)

Musical · Linguistic · Naturalist · Interpersonal · Intrapersonal · Visual · Mathematical · Kinesthetic

Why not audit your own teaching and put the results next to your MI profile?

Natalie was quick to act. She was missing opportunities to reach learners with strengths different from hers; she needed more bodily and musical activities. But rather than plug in a rap and a role play, together we hit on an idea for combining any two intelligences: MI twins (two intelligences).

ACTIVITY

Alone: Decide on the intelligences you will pair as MI twins. Use one intelligence as a stimulus to learning, another to express understanding (bodily/kinesthetic and musical/rhythmic are in this example).

With your learners:

1. Define your learning objective, for example: To know and use a range of adjectives.

2. Select two target intelligences – musical (1) and bodily (2).

3. Organize your learners into two equal groups (A and B) and send group B out of the room, with a learning assistant, if available.

4. Use intelligence 1 as a stimulus for group A. Group A listen to a piece of classical music, thinking about which adjectives from a list they would use to describe it. Loud? Frightening? Peaceful? Jumpy?

5. Ask group A to use intelligence 2 to express the adjectives they chose. Group A create facial expressions and poses – shouting face, hunched and scared, sleeping, shivering.

6. Invite group B back into the room and form A + B pairs.

7. Group A children use intelligence 2 to present the learning objective to Bs, repeating the expressions and poses.

8. Bs try to describe the original stimulus (intelligence 1). 'Was it a creepy piece of music?' 'Was it slow – you were asleep, weren't you?'

9. Repeat the original stimulus to both groups and discuss how accurately the ideas were transferred.

MI twins can be simplified by keeping the class together and having everyone express the stimulus through the second intelligence or by linking the stimulus directly to the learning objective. For example:

- Use a painting as a stimulus for a quotation.
- Use a diary entry as a stimulus for a song.
- Use a poem as a stimulus for a clay model.

Alone: A pair of six-sided dice can give you a quick way to generate a further 36 ideas for MI twins – nearly one every week for a whole teaching year. Throw the dice to select one from each column in the table over the page. For example, if you throw a 2 and a 6, use a poem to inspire model-making.

MI twin generator			
	Use a...		as stimulus for a...
⚀	song	⚀	song
⚁	poem	⚁	poem
⚂	quotation	⚂	quotation
⚃	diary entry	⚃	diary entry
⚄	painting	⚄	painting
⚅	model	⚅	model

The products/outcomes in the second column are inspired by MI and can be altered, or extended to generate even more MI twins. But beware, there are a lot of possible twins out there... nine intelligences... many products related to each one... Some form of birth control may be needed! By reflecting on her practice, Natalie created a simple idea to help her provide a broader range of learning activities.

Day 40   9.15 PM

1 2 3 4 5 6 7 8 9 10 11 12 13 14 15 16 17 18 19 20 21 22 23 24 25 26 27 28 29 30 31

Wow! What a day! This morning the children and I did something completely different in literacy. We completed the activity using the musical and kinesthetic intelligences. The children responded really well. We even evaluated the lesson at the end as a class and recorded our comments under positive, minus and interesting aspects. It was great to get the feedback from the children and they appreciated our comments too. (My TA added in her comments.) The children used the bank of powerful adjectives and verbs to assist them in writing their fighting scene in their Greek myth. It is definitely something I'll consider using again.

Day 45   9.20 PM

1 2 3 4 5 6 7 8 9 10 11 12 13 14 15 16 17 18 19 20 21 22 23 24 25 26 27 28 29 30 31

The children looked back at their original profiles and to find out who had the same strong intelligences as them. It helps me too to find out how to use my strongest intelligences and which I need to improve.

Becoming an MI teacher

Your intelligences profile will influence your teaching strategies. You may need to develop some in order to match your students' or class's MI profile. Here are some ideas for growing your teaching in different directions.

Intelligence	Teaching strategies
Verbal/linguistic	• Explain in words and lectures • Provide opportunities to read, write, speak, listen, persuade, inform, debate • Tell stories • Share your linguistic talents and hobbies with your learners (Poetry? Acting?)
Logical/mathematical	• Provide opportunities to reason, enquire, evaluate and analyse • Make connections between concepts • Explain the steps of a lesson at the beginning • Share your logical talents and hobbies (Mental maths? Sudoku? Logic puzzles?)
Musical/rhythmic	• Use sound, voice and music to enhance presentations, projects and learning environments • Provide opportunities to compose and appreciate music and rhythm • Make connections between music and other subjects • Share your musical talents and hobbies (Singing? Guitar?)
Visual/spatial	• Provide opportunities for looking and watching – videos/photographs/diagrams • Use mind mapping • Use visual language: 'I see what you mean', 'It looks OK to me', 'Let me paint a picture for you' • Share your visual talents and hobbies (Art? Photography?)
Interpersonal	• Encourage collaborative group-work and discussion • Model emotional intelligence • Show an interest in learners' lives outside school • Share your life outside school with your learners
Intrapersonal	• Provide opportunities for learners to work independently • Reflect on, audit and develop your teaching • Use regular goal setting, progress reports and reflection times in class • Remember to share some of your thoughts with your learners
Bodily/kinesthetic	• Provide opportunities to move • Explain concepts with hand movements • Use bodily language: 'You'll get a feel for it', 'Get a move on!' • Share your bodily talents and hobbies (Sport? 3D art?)

Existential	• Ask questions such as 'Why?' and 'How?' • Challenge beliefs • Provide opportunities for extended thinking, such as P4C (Philosophy for Children) • Share your existential talents and hobbies (Philosophy? Spirituality?)
Naturalist	• Provide opportunities for outdoor study visits and field trips • Draw attention to features of the natural world • Present information in hierarchies and taxonomies • Share your naturalist talents/hobbies with your learners (Gardening? Walking?)

As you embrace MI theory and expand your repertoire of teaching strategies, general characteristics will emerge. Some of them are listed in the activity below.

ACTIVITY

Alone: Tick the statements that apply to you, and repeat every term to see how you're growing. If you're just starting out with MI, don't worry if you tick only one or two statements first time round.

As an MI teacher, I...

☐ believe that all students are intelligent in unique ways

☐ believe that intelligence is multifaceted and dynamic

☐ have a good understanding of MI theory

☐ use intelligences as alternative routes to specific curriculum areas

☐ use MI to identify and nurture specific talents

☐ use students' stronger intelligences to teach weaker areas

☐ give students choices of activity

☐ use MI to model real-world problem solving

☐ have a good knowledge of students' intelligence profiles

☐ understand how MI theory relates to the school curriculum

☐ present learning material in a style that engages most or all of the intelligences

☐ encourage student self-reflection

☐ enrich assessment activities to include evaluation through intelligences other than linguistic.

Teaching and learning *to* MI – the 'building on strengths' pathway

In *Multiple Intelligences in the Elementary Classroom*, Julie Viens defines 'building on strengths' as a pathway into literacy (though it can be equally well applied to other areas):

● to support literacy development

● to 'bridge' student strengths to literacy learning.

I once heard of a group of Russian educators in England who came across the National Literacy Strategy. They commented that not even in Stalin's day was anything so rigorously and mechanically disseminated down through a country's hierarchy.

Love or hate it, the Strategy stayed, and now it's being unravelled by initiatives such as *Excellence and Enjoyment* – allowing creative teachers to meet its worthy learning aims in a variety of ways.

The following case study shows how MI can be used within the original NLS framework, in an enriched Literacy Hour that:

● presents experience of text in a variety of ways

● provides different activities for the same learning objective

● matches learner strengths to type of activity

● offers learners other activities for the same objective.

Case study

Resource : An intelligent Literacy Hour
Teacher : Mike Fleetham
Location : Fernhurst Junior School, Portsmouth

This Year 3 lesson was introduced by saying that the text focus was rhyming poetry ('My Future' by David Harmer). It had been explored for a day or two already. The poem questions the sort of future we are making for our children (existential, naturalist).

'I modelled the reading, drawing attention to features such as rhyme and punctuation. Then children read it together. The OHT had a green and blue Earth-like tint, and there was music to support the meaning ('Low Light' from Peter Gabriel's Ovo). Linguistic, visual and musical intelligences had already been awakened.

'To look at intonation I drew on the bodily intelligence. The children moved their hands up and down with the tone of their voices. Then they chose their favourite phrase and justified their choice to the child next to them (interpersonal). Finally, we did a line count and looked for the rhyming pattern (logical).

'Link to word work was a focus on the long a vowel sound. I began a mind map using coloured pens. We found several ways of making long a, a few examples of each, and considered exceptions to the rules.

'This led directly into group-work. The children are grouped by one of their strongest intelligences and work on the learning objective at different intelligence areas in the room. For example, the intrapersonal children worked alone to extend the mind map; interpersonals work at the flip chart with dictionaries to collect as many long a words as they could; the BKs (bodily/kinesthetics) made words with plasticine; visual children were doing guided reading, looking at illustrations for similar poems and then visualizing with eyes closed.

'In the plenary, musical students performed a short song they made with the teaching assistant. It included eight long a words and a strong rhythm.

'The following day in group-work, the children moved to a different intelligence area. They worked to the same learning outcome, but used different intelligences. Their dominant learning route is honoured while lesser paths are developed.'

Here are some comments that children have made about such lessons:

'I like the music in the background for our shared text.'

'We sit down and get all our intelligences going.'

'When we do shared text we have music and we move our hands and that makes it fun.'

'I like sitting with my intelligence group because they help me, but sometimes they are annoying.'

'We are the linguistic group and the good thing is we can listen well, but sometimes we use our mouths too much.'

'Being in a group of intelligences is a good thing but the bad thing is maybe you don't have a friend in your group.'

'We shouldn't put all the BKs together… we should work in different groups so we can learn different intelligences. Then it's fun.'

Planning

The extract from a weekly plan, opposite, shows how MI can be used in literacy. The 'MI' column is a checklist reminding you to include different types of activity. You don't have to use every intelligence in every lesson, but keeping track should reveal an even spread over time. The 'MI group' column is an abbreviated list of MI groups – learners organized by one of their strongest intelligences. The 'Activity' column next to it lists a carousel of tasks, each using a different intelligence. Each group moves on one activity every day, starting with a task matched to their strengths. After a week's rotation, everyone has used their strengths and had a chance to develop their weaknesses.

Text focus: Instructions

Sentence focus: Verbs

Word focus: Apostrophe for contractions

Texts: *Clockwork* (Pullman); various instructional; student cookbook

	Whole-class work/group-work			Inter/intrapersonal group-work			Plenary
	Objectives	MI activity	MI	Objective	MI group	Activity	
Mon	Identify 2 uses of inst texts	Share texts; categorize; tally; make hand code; sing syllables.	vis	Use illus to support text	inter	Guided: Cover text, guess text, use pictures	'I can...' – Inters
	Read, say, write and understand meaning of 9 new words	Visualize 5s/say 5x/write in air 5x/visualize; cover, write, check	mus	Chant-read texts	intra	Guided: Colour every other word	
			BK	Follow 2-part instructions	vis & mus	Paired: Follow and use verbal instructions	
			mat	Syllabify words	BK	Make syllable code for spellings	
			nat	Link word meanings	ling	Make link map for spellings	
Tues	Identify 5+ uses of inst texts	Repeat previous hand code; read recipe and act with eyes closed (to jazz)	vis	Use illus to support text	vis & mus	Guided: Cover text, guess text, use pictures	'I can' – Intras
	Identify and categorize 1st, 2nd & 3rd person in text	Make body code for 1st, 2nd & 3rd person; identify and tally 1st, 2nd & 3rd person in *Clockwork*	mus	Chant-read text	BK	Guided: Colour every other word	
			BK	Follow 2-part instructions	ling	Paired: Follow and use verbal instructions	
			mat	Syllabify words	inter	Make syllable code for spellings	
			nat	Link word meanings	intra	Make link map for spellings	

Once you have planned your MI literacy lessons, the table below provides some ideas of how you can use MI to get into a shared text. (Some of the suggestions will require the children to use mini-whiteboards.)

Intelligence	Shared text activity
Verbal/linguistic	• Listen for keywords in the text – tallying these as they are heard • Write down certain types of word from the text – three-letter/verbs/adjectives • Two groups read a sentence or a line alternately
Logical/mathematical	• Count up the number of particular words or letters in the text • Use a Venn diagram to represent certain aspects of the text • Make a flow chart of the text
Musical/rhythmic	• Use a soundtrack – music or sounds that support the meanings of the text • Emphasize the rhythm in the text • Model and encourage intonation
Visual/spatial	• Provide images or objects to support the meaning(s) of the text • Mind map the meaning/flow of the text • Close eyes and visualize the meaning of the text
Interpersonal	• Paired discussion about specific aspects of the text • Emphasize emotions in the text • Read text all together in sync
Intrapersonal	• Use own copies of the text • Give time to reflect alone on the text • Write personal response to the text
Bodily/kinesthetic	• Use finger movements and sounds to punctuate text (see facing page) • Move hands up and down to indicate intonation or the text theme • Make human tableaux to illustrate aspects of text
Existential	• Explore deeper meanings – ask 'Why?', 'How?' and 'What does this say about life?' • Give thinking and pondering time
Naturalist	• Relate the text to nature • Organize the text's words into a hierarchy: top layer – all words; next layer – verbs/nouns/adjectives/adverbs; and so on • Read in a different place from normal

These actions and sounds can be useful to punctuate a text. Feel free to change them – your learners will have lots of ideas.

Punctuation mark	'Finger/hand in the air' action	Sound
.	Poke	Single 'cluck' with tongue
?	Draw a question mark (finishing with a poke)	Curious wondering sound followed by 'cluck'
!	Draw an exclamation mark (plus poke)	'Whooo' followed by 'cluck'
" "	Two fingers make rabbit ears	Rabbit sound (like a rabbit eating a carrot)
,	Flick down with vertical, finger	'Shush'
/	Karate chop	'Ha'
( )	Both hands make brackets	'Ahhhhh'
...	Three pokes	'Da, da, da'
;	Finger and thumb poke then flick	'Cluck–shush'
:	Finger and thumb poke, poke	'Cluck cluck'

There's a really useful question you can ask to measure the impact of MI on their literacy learning. You need ask it only twice; once on the first day of the year, and again on the last: 'How many ways are there to learn spellings?'

Most primary classes will answer with, 'Look, Cover, Say, Write, Check' (or a regional variation on that theme). This does generally do the trick, but the following is the list one of my classes came up with after a year of exposure to MI:

● **Musical**: Tape them, set them to music, clap them, sing them, dance them, play them on an instrument, make different sounds mean different letters.

● **Verbal**: Read them, write them, say them, listen to them, look them up, write them in sentences, play consequences with them.

● **Interpersonal**: Let your partner test you, throw a paper aeroplane to your partner when they spell it right, with the words on the wings, play charades.

● **Intrapersonal**: Write a learning journal and a personal dictionary, give me peace and quiet, mark my own work, set my own targets, be a one-person spellchecker.

- **Visual**: Put the words on a tray – look at them – cover them, remove one – which one's gone?, read and write them upside down, imagine them, use bubble writing, find patterns, write them big/in colour/with glitter.

- **Logical**: Make a word puzzle, count the letters, make secret codes, do anagrams, find letter patterns, number words – roll a dice to know which one to spell, do a flow chart.

- **Bodily**: Cut them out of card, use chalk, make them with multi-link, act them out, finger-draw them, write them in sand or in window condensation, make them with plasticine, move different bits of your body for different letters or words.

That's around 50 ideas. The sad thing was that the following year this class went back to Look, Say, Cover, Write, Check.

Evidence

Debates about 'new' teaching methods such as MI and learning styles usually come down to evidence: can it be proved that MI will improve standards? This is difficult evidence to collect; not because teachers don't believe MI works, but because it's difficult to link improvement to a single factor. There can be so many influences and initiatives in a classroom that it's hard to separate out what causes what.

The first year I taught literacy with MI, I found that average reading grades went up a National Curriculum sub-level more that an equivalent parallel class. That year's class came on more than my previous year's (who didn't get any MI), and I was able to repeat this modest improvement the following year. Does this prove MI works? Yes from my perspective, but generally no. It worked for me in a particular school with a particular set of learners, but that's no guarantee that it will work elsewhere.

By now you probably do believe in MI and the benefits it can bring, but you need to build your own store of evidence. So, while the policy makers and educational press debate MI, if it works for you, adapt it, organize evidence for it and make it your own.

Teaching and learning *to* MI – the 'talent development' pathway

This pathway is especially relevant in three key areas:

- Specialist colleges

- Gifted, able and talented provision

- Careers.

Specialist schools

Specialist secondary schools focus on a chosen subject and provide enhanced learning opportunities in this area. There are several specialist areas: arts, business and enterprise, engineering, humanities, language, maths and computing, music, science, sports and technology. There is some general correspondence between these areas and the intelligences.

Schools can opt to teach two specialist subjects, such as science and engineering, but must meet the requirements of the National Curriculum to deliver a wide and balanced range of subjects. This can be done by infusing the specialist subject into the other areas. See www.specialistschools.org.uk.

From 1998, specialist schools have been permitted to select up to ten per cent of their student intake on the basis of 'aptitude' for the specialist subject. Stephen Byers, education minister at the time, distinguished 'aptitude' from ability by defining it as a question of potential rather than current capacity. This implies that some children may well end up in a secondary school totally mismatched to their skills and talents. Specialist schools can therefore make use of MI in three ways:

1. Identify which students have an 'aptitude' for the school's speciality (and which don't).

2. Use MI to infuse the speciality into other subject areas.

3. Use MI to enrich teaching strategies for the speciality.

A specialist sports college, for example, could use MI to identify learners at either end of the bodily/kinesthetic scale. Intrapersonal and interpersonal scales are also important – they indicate dispositions towards dedication, motivation and teamwork – key to sporting success. The college could also use MI to give a 'BK' spin to other subjects: sport/games-based investigations, calculations, poems, artwork, songs, stories, debates, comedy routines, videos, and so on. And finally, teachers without a sports speciality could use MI to master alternative teaching strategies.

Gifted, able and talented provision

The labels of 'gifted', 'talented' and 'able' are used variously across the country to describe learners who excel in specific subjects. I've come across many interesting and different ways of identifying such learners, including:

● problem-solving ability

● literacy and numeracy scores

● neatness of handwriting

● behaviour

● off-the-wall-ness of answers.

It almost goes without saying that each of the above is either a restrictive, misleading, inaccurate or unfair method of identifying excellence. A thorough MI profiling system will quickly identify learners who excel in one area. A rich MI environment and curriculum will provide the opportunities they need.

Careers

If you're of roughly middle age, you may remember a special piece of careers advice given to you at secondary school. Several weeks after answering a questionnaire, you were presented with a huge strip of computer printout paper (the wide stuff with green lines and holes down each edge) on which an analysis of your answers produced (eventually, on the final page) your ideal career. My three top recommendations were:

1. Nurse

2. Geologist

3. Film director.

I have so far enjoyed my working life as an engineer, teacher and now consultant and author. Though I do have some plans...

If you remember the Department of New Intelligences on pages 38–40, you might recall that one of Howard Gardner's criteria for an intelligence is: 'a distinctive developmental history, along with a definable set of "end-state" performances.'

These 'end-state' performances are the careers to which an MI profile can be matched. As learners move through their education, it can be helpful to know if their talents suit their dream job, and if not, what needs to be worked on. Although all careers require a mix of skills, the following can be seen to have a dominant intelligence trait:

Politician, writer, negotiator, counsellor, poet	Verbal/linguistic
Scientist, mathematician, cryptologist, detective	Logical/mathematical
Singer, musician, composer, record producer	Musical/rhythmic
Film director, photographer, artist	Visual/spatial
Sports star, actor, dancer, sculptor	Bodily/kinesthetic
Teacher, manager, helpdesk operator, counsellor	Interpersonal
Explorer, athlete	Intrapersonal
Philosopher, religious leader, healer/complimentary therapist	Existential
Marine biologist, environmentalist, zoologist, vet	Naturalist

Teaching and learning *through* MI – the 'understanding' pathway

Baum, Viens and Slatin say that this pathway can be more learner-centred, less intelligence-specific or both:

'In the "understanding" pathway, multiple intelligences theory is used to enhance and diversify how topics and concepts are approached. Students are given opportunities to access and understand material, as well as to demonstrate their understanding, in ways that align with their areas of strengths and interest.'

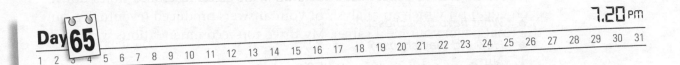

7.20 pm

Today was a brilliant day. We have been studying the Trojan Horse as part of our Ancient Greece topic. I was thinking of how the children could think and learn about the Trojan Horse using some of the intelligences. I came up with this (based on when the soldiers come out of the horse): linguistic had a picture of the horse and had to write the story to go with it; visual had a description of the horse and had to draw a picture; musical had a description and had to create a piece of music; kinesthetic had to act the scene; logical had to create a list of instructions on how to make a Trojan Horse. It worked so well and the children really enjoyed looking at what the others had been up to. I'm going to adapt this for other subjects.

Capturing learners' interests

Look at the top ten of any children's book list and it will be full of imaginary worlds, thanks to the linguistic skills of authors such as G.P. Taylor, Philip Pullman, Garth Nix and J.K. Rowling. Their engaging stories often appear on the big screen and give imaginary worlds a prime position in children's literary experience.

Teachers at Front Lawn Junior School wanted to develop learner independence, choice-making and responsibility. They decided to do this through MI and their literacy work on imaginary worlds.

Case study

Resource : Using MI to teach imaginary worlds
Teachers : Tina, Barbie and Davina
Location : Front Lawn Junior School, Havant

The plan began with multisensory stimuli: websites, visualization, artwork, reading, music, role play – raising awareness of different 'invented places'. The teachers offered several activities, one of which could be chosen:

- *Action – role play, drama or dance*
- *Quiet zone – for thinking, writing, drawing, quiet conversation*
- *Music making – instruments, songwriting*
- *Clay – 3D model making*
- *Building – blocks/construction kit*
- *Art – sketching/pastels.*

Once the children had chosen and set to work, the adults recorded:

- What have they chosen?
- How did they choose?
- Are they working independently?
- Have they chosen to work alone or with others?
- Are individuals happy to specialize in one activity?

By the end of the activities, teachers noted that everyone had been able to work independently, behaviour was better than normal and the children had been very quick to organize themselves and start work.

Children's comments on the activities above included:

'I enjoyed being independent because we can let our brilliant, colourful imaginations run free. We don't need to worry if we do something wrong.'

'It was fun building your imaginary world. I liked working with my partner.'

'I chose clay-making to create the Valley of Green Doom.'

'I chose art to bring my world to life with reflecting salt water.'

'I chose the quiet area for drawing, writing and poetry.'

The example above comes from primary school, though such approaches are not confined to it. Trish Raper from Milton Cross Secondary School in Portsmouth has used the 'understanding' pathway in drama. Here is one of her lesson plans for a mixed-ability Year 7 class, which clearly gives students an opportunity to learn in a range of ways.

Drama topic: the Mary Celeste	
Intelligence	**Task**
Intrapersonal	• Conduct individual research into the Bermuda Triangle and the *Mary Celeste* using books and the internet
Logical/mathematical	• Produce a flow chart analysis of what you think happened to the *Mary Celeste*
Verbal/linguistic	• Write a news report shortly after the ship's disappearance • Create a court scene with Captain Briggs, his wife and daughter and some of the crew. Each prepares a short speech to the court about where they were and what happened to them. The court can ask questions • Write a poem entitled 'Last Trip on the *Mary Celeste*'
Musical/rhythmic	• Study sea shanties with the class and set groups the task of producing one of their own • Use a range of percussion instruments, to represent the creation and dissipation of a sea storm

Visual/spatial	• Draw a plan of the *Mary Celeste* indicating where all the clues to the crew's disappearance were found • Design a poster requesting information to help solve the mystery
Interpersonal	• Interview members of the boarding party who discovered the ship • Create a modern-day TV programme about the ship's disappearance, containing interviews with relatives of the crew and experts on the Bermuda Triangle
Bodily/kinesthetic	• Make various improvisations of parts of the story. A particularly successful one is the scene at Captain Briggs' last meal, still on the table when the ship was discovered. The improvisation should end when something significant is about to happen • Create a freeze-frame of the party boarding the *Mary Celeste* and discovering no one. Add an in-role thought by each member
Naturalist	• Consider the theories about the crew's disappearance relating to seabirds and sea monsters. Research the type of marine life to be found in the area. Present findings, including drawings, to the rest of the class

Teachers at Goldsmith Infant School in Portsmouth take the 'understanding' pathway into all aspects of teaching and learning, but they began with a simple MI register time.

Case study

Resource : MI register
Teacher : Alison Spittles, headteacher
Location : Goldsmith Infant School, Portsmouth

Each registration method below was taught to the children over a week. They then decided for themselves which way to respond for the rest of the term.

- *Musical – clap rhythm of name, sing name.*
- *Logical – put name card in the red hoop, teacher puts absentees' cards in the blue hoop; use Venn sorting by other criteria (has had breakfast/feels happy/both; is a boy/has done homework/both).*
- *Bodily – nod/wave/stand.*
- *Interpersonal – answer with, 'Good morning, everyone.'*
- *Intrapersonal – say, '1', '2' or '3', based on how happy you are.*
- *Visual – place laminated mini self-portrait on the board.*
- *Verbal – write name or initials on whiteboard/say name.*
- *Naturalist – answer as a different animal/register outside.*

Alison Spittles says, 'From a very small start we were able to evaluate the benefits in children's engagement and the subsequent improvement in behaviour.

Immediately, significant observation and assessment opportunities were available to us and we began to consider the need for profiling on entry to ensure that we had a deeper understanding of pupils' inherent preferences and areas for development. We believe that the profile impacts significantly on our knowledge of our pupils and the work we undertake with them.

'Our curriculum is appropriately differentiated, not just in relation to previously understood "intelligence" but across the board, with opportunities for the children to engage in a range of activities specifically planned to develop all intelligences.'

Before they can follow the 'understanding' pathway, learners need to know that there are many ways to learn the same thing. They also need to know that it's alright to learn something in a different way. A little MI, often, at register time, is a superb way to teach them this, as are school assemblies.

Case study

Resource : MI-inspired assemblies
Teacher : Debbie Anderson, headteacher
Location : College Park Infant School, Portsmouth

'One of the first things that struck me in my new school was how passive the children were. I resolved to make my assemblies less boring! Not to mention wanting to appeal to all and ensure that everyone got something out of the experience.

'During the Easter holidays, I worked with a fellow headteacher to take MI into account and fully consider the needs of the children in an act of collective worship. We had the following ideas:

- *Children or staff acting out mini dramas.*
- *Leader dressed up or in role.*
- *Chanting, refrains or repetitive sequences.*
- *Written or drawn responses, adults scribing for children.*
- *Talking or sharing ideas with a partner/person next to you.*
- *Quiz/game format.*
- *Giving whole-school compliments with contributions from staff and children.*
- *Rewarding individuals (pupils or staff) with stickers or certificates linked to the assembly focus.*
- *Actions and facial expressions linked to words.*
- *Making up songs and poems to familiar tunes.*
- *Use of feely bags and puppets.*
- *PowerPoint presentations.*
- *Making lists of ideas.*
- *Contributions for a display.*
- *Sitting a class or year group in a different place.*
- *Leading the assembly from a different place, including outdoors.*

- *Having a child or member of staff say a spontaneous prayer.*
- *Varying the music for coming in/going out.*
- *Changing the focus for reflection (music, image, prop, symbol).*

'Many of these ideas are not new, but what was significant for us was the systematic way in which we incorporated these strategies to involve all pupils in our assemblies.

'It did break up the tedium and encouraged pupils (and staff) to be more interested in sharing in the whole-school experience. My Year 2s loved playing Who Wants to be a Millionaire? *with one of them sat in my office chair during the assembly. The other children were the audience, and the staff the 'phone a friend' option. Instead of prize money, stickers and certificates in growing size and worth were offered. It was great!*

'It was a gamble to ask the children to reflect on an assembly and then tell them that one of them would be saying a prayer that they had just made up. The staff looked horrified, but it was a moment of pure wonder. K spoke so beautifully that I wanted to cry.

'I have to admit that it does take longer to plan assemblies with an awareness of MI, but it is really worth it. Even when you just read a story like 'Toffee the Golden Labrador' [from Join With Us Book 1 *by Jeanne L. Jackson] when exploring the theme of caring for animals, it is possible to have a real spiritual moment simply because reading a story is not what you always do.*

'I'm looking forward to growing an amaryllis in my assemblies after Christmas for my pupils who are naturalist, making up a new school song for those who are musical and asking a visual child to draw their interpretation of red when I get to the theme of colour, light and sound.'

MI and thinking skills

Deep and thorough understanding comes when subject matter is experienced, processed and expressed in ways matched to the learner's needs. The experiencing bit is more to do with learning styles, the expressing bit favours multiple intelligences and the processing bit relates to thinking skills.

The National Curriculum for Key Stages 2 and 3 identifies six areas of thinking skill:

- Information processing
- Reasoning
- Enquiry
- Creativity
- Evaluation
- Metacognition (thinking about thinking).

There are over 50 further hierarchies and taxonomies of thinking skill. One of the best known is Bloom's Taxonomy.

In 1956, educational theorist and teacher Benjamin Bloom chaired a committee of college and university examiners whose task was to discover how students thought as they learned and to classify the different levels of thinking they found. This table shows how the taxonomy works, using wine as an example to think about.

Level of taxonomy	Which means...	Example
Knowledge	Finding out	I know about wine
Comprehension	Understanding	I can explain wine to you
Application	Making use of the knowledge	I can use wine
Analysis	Taking apart what is known	I can consider the issues around wine
Synthesis	Putting things together in another way	I can create low-alcohol wine
Evaluation	Judging what happens	I can judge wine against vodka

Now move away from the taxonomy/hierarchy view and give your various learners opportunities to think at all levels. You can do this by asking different sorts of questions and by providing different sorts of activities. For example:

Level of thinking	Typical skills
Knowledge	Remember, name, observe, identify, describe, find
Comprehension	Explain, summarize, interpret, retell, order, relate
Application	Use, apply, solve, choose, change, produce, make
Analysis	Investigate, take apart, examine, distinguish, classify, categorize
Synthesis	Invent, create, combine, hypothesize, plan, imagine
Evaluation	Assess, criticize, value, judge, compare, choose

Mary Sefton, music advisory teacher from Bracknell Forest LEA, has combined Bloom's Taxonomy with multiple intelligences to produce a rich mosaic of learning opportunities, shown in the example in the table on the opposite page.

The MI columns (2–8) give possible activities – a bank of ideas – to include during a music topic on animals. Column 9 gives six learning objectives to address during the topic and ensures coverage of all Bloom's levels. The final column lists the activities that the teacher has decided to use – chosen from the idea bank.

Animal magic

Blooms \ MI	Verbal/linguistic	Logical/mathematical	Visual/spatial	Bodily/kinesthetic	Musical	Interpersonal	Intrapersonal	Learning objective	Chosen activity
Knowledge	Explain musical elements used in 'Trust in Me' from The Jungle Book	Analyse the structure of the piece	Draw a simple graphic score showing the structure	Move in response to the music	Listen to 'Trust in Me' from The Jungle Book	Discuss as a class how music communicates ideas/images	Begin log about the feelings/images from the music	To identify features of a piece of music and how it communicates mood	Listen to a recording of 'Trust in Me' from The Jungle Book
Comprehension	Explain how the musical elements help to portray the character of the snake	Use information of animal movement and create rhythms to match movements	Make a collage of rainforest animals under headings 'tempo' and 'dynamics'	Choose instruments to represent animals, and move to their sound	Sing song conveying the character of the music	Work with a partner on creating sounds and movements to reflect an animal	Discuss with a partner how you felt on completing the task	To be able to sing confidently and tunefully	Sing the song 'Trust in Me'
Application	Write phrases to describe different animals	Organize music into a structure, deciding upon length	Play the piece, ensuring a good sound	Perform piece to rest of class	Compose a short piece about an animal (within group)	Agree on a group leader/conductor	Reflect upon your contribution to the composition	To use musical elements to create a piece of music	Within a group compose a short piece of music
Analysis	Discuss aspects of the composition with group members	Organize music to have a definite beat or pulse	Draw graphic score of animal composition, showing musical instructions in some way	Develop a dance about the animal	Revise/extend music in the light of comments	Class discussion about compositions and how they could be developed further	Improvise to develop ideas to fit into the group's overall plan	To refine ideas and explore movements	Revise and extend ideas; devise movements relating to music
Synthesis	Within the group agree on two ways to improve or develop the piece and give reasons	Play the music in a different way, e.g. using different instruments, changing the dynamics	Play the piece following the graphic score	Perform dance ensuring relationship to music	Perform music relating to dance movement	Listen to contributions and act accordingly	Take turns conducting group	To consolidate relationship between music and movement; to perform the piece	Work towards a final performance
Evaluation	Write programme notes about the piece	How does this change the mood of the music?	Evaluate how well the graphic score represented the music	Reflect upon how the dance movements correspond to music	Record composition and evaluate the musical content	Discuss as a group, agree on one positive area of composition and one area for development	Reflect upon how contribution developed the composition	To evaluate the methods used and the final performance	Write an evaluation

MI assessment with the 'understanding' pathway

A good friend of mine has recently completed her MEd. One of her assignments was on formative assessment – assessment for learning – receiving quality feedback leading into the next learning experience (rather than assessment of learning – receiving a grade).

She put a great deal of effort into her project – researching, visiting schools, reading up on best practice, trying out ideas, and finally submitted what she thought was an acceptable piece. A few weeks later she collected it and eagerly turned to the back page to read comments – how had she done? Which ideas were good? Which ones should she revisit? What was her presentation/style like?

But on the back page, there was only a number: 54. Double disappointment. Not only were there no formative comments, but she didn't even know how many the 54 was out of, and she never found out.

One of the keys to successful formative assessment is to involve learners in the process. MI provides many alternative ways to assess learning – writing, role play and photographs are all equally valuable – and lets learners show what they know by using what they're good at. If someone excels visually, let them show what they know with images rather than words; if someone is strong linguistically, let them speak and write rather than sing. Here are some straightforward examples.

Intelligence	Example of assessment
Musical	Song or jingle
Linguistic	Written test
Naturalist	Any classification work (such as a key)
Interpersonal	Contribution to group discussion
Intrapersonal	Diary
Visual	Diagram or piece of artwork
Mathematical	Flow chart, Venn diagram
Bodily	Dance, drama, role play

A powerful implementation of formative assessment comes when learners assess their peers against agreed criteria. Here's how that could sound – if the children had developed the skills needed to work at this level:

'Well done, I liked your song. It was eight lines long, with a chorus; you sung in tune and included three ideas from our topic on the Romans. Next time it would be great to have some accompaniment – maybe a drum.'

Teaching and learning *through* MI: the 'authentic problems' pathway

The final pathway looks at creativity and at how multiple intelligences can be used in the real world. Baum, Viens and Slatin say that the 'authentic problems' pathway works like this:

'This pathway uses MI theory as a framework for implementing authentic, problem-based learning experiences. In essence this pathway tries to simulate the 'real world' experience of intelligences in action by providing real or realistic problems to solve. In these learning situations students assume the role of the practicing professional and use authentic means to solve problems and develop products. They become budding engineers, sculptors, actors, or poets in the classroom, and their products are used to communicate their creative solutions to problems they encountered. Learning becomes relevant through real world contexts. Basic skills are developed in authentic situations.'

MI and creative problem solving

I was working with a group of Year 2 children earlier in the year, tapping into their creativity. They were studying pirates, so I told them about a ship's cat I'd once met who used to climb up into the crow's-nest. The crew were annoyed about this because the cat was supposed to be on deck catching mice and rats. 'How can they get the cat down?' I asked.

After a bit of thinking time the children came up with four or five really good answers – call out to it, shake the mast, throw water at it, and so on. I then told them about the different intelligences and asked them the same question.

They amazed me by coming up with over 40 different ideas! For each intelligence they came up with five or so ideas – combined they had eight times as many, for example:

- Sing the cat to sleep and hope it falls off.
- Make a loud noise to scare it down.
- Get a lady cat to sit at the bottom of the mast. (I'm not sure where she comes from, but you get the idea.)
- Put a fish at the bottom of the mast.
- Climb up and get it. (Obviously!)
- Lasso it.
- Persuade it down. (It's a hearing-talking cat.)
- Get a mast-climbing dog to chase it down.
- Put a picture of a fish at the bottom of the mast.
- Throw a fish at it.
- Make a human pyramid and the top sailor gets it.

I would love to claim the credit for inventing this innovative and engaging use of multiple intelligences, but credit goes to Cheryl Garlinge, a primary teacher from Slough. The following case study shows how Cheryl has created an activity that offers opportunities to meet learning objectives, in literacy or design and technology for example, by using multiple intelligences creatively.

Case study

Resource : Using MI for creative problem solving —
'How to rescue a princess' group task
Teacher : Cheryl Garlinge
Location : Baylis Court School, Slough

There are several tried-and-tested ways to rescue a princess from a dragon. Cheryl Garlinge has used MI theory to increase the quantity and quality of possible approaches to this task. Her class is organized into problem-solving groups, each group being allocated one dominant intelligence with which to tackle the princess' predicament:

'A beautiful princess is forced to live all by herself in a tall tower that is surrounded by a deep moat. She is kept a prisoner in the tower by a fierce, fire-breathing dragon. You are the brave and handsome prince. You must decide as a typical group of intelligent learners the most unusual and original way to rescue her. Be prepared to report back on your plans.'

One group has been asked to think using the musical intelligence. Solutions may include:

- *Play a lullaby to make the dragon fall asleep.*
- *Get the princess to sing to the dragon so that he falls in love with her and has to let her go.*
- *Tap annoyingly on your shield so that the dragon gets really irritated and goes away.*
- *Involve the dragon in a song and while he's distracted, grab the princess and run away.*

The use of MI works well here because it supports creativity: it can be daunting to think up an 'unusual and original idea' – especially if you aren't an 'ideas person'. MI provides starting points, boundaries and a structure for thinking.

Creative problem solving with multiple intelligences can be used to introduce, consolidate or review learning in any topic and for any age group. The table opposite gives some examples linked to different subjects. It's a good idea to set such challenges twice: first without MI, then repeated using MI thinking. That way, your learners will be able to appreciate the difference.

Subject	Problem
English	An author is suffering from writer's block. He needs ideas for his next book.
Maths	Where can maths be used to solve problems?
Science	What would you most like to discover or invent?
History	A character from history has been imprisoned underground. How can she escape?
Geography	An island has been cut off from civilization, including food supplies. How can the inhabitants survive and re-establish contact?
D&T	You can construct any machine you like. What would you make?
RE	Invent a new religion.
PE	Invent a new sport.
ICT	All the computers in the world have started talking to each other and plotting against humanity. How can you defend yourselves?
PSHE	Two friends have just been moved on from the town centre by the police. How can they occupy their time legally and creatively and have fun too?
A&D	You are a successful but bored painter. What new art forms could you turn your hand to?
Music	Cylinder, vinyl, tape, mini-disk, CD, mp3 – what forms of music media will there be in the next 100 years?
Dance	You have to perform a dance to an audience of 1,000 people who don't like dance. What can you do?
Drama	An actor has started to forget his lines. How can you help him to remember them?
MFL	You are stuck in a country whose language you don't know. How could you go about learning it?
Media	A production company has asked you to come up with original ideas for a new reality TV programme. Create.
Food tech	A leisure group has asked you to come up with original ideas for a new themed restaurant. Create.

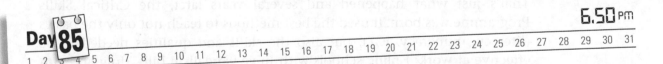

Day 85   6.50 pm

1 2 3 4 5 6 7 8 9 10 11 12 13 14 15 16 17 18 19 20 21 22 23 24 25 26 27 28 29 30 31

We've just had Creativity Week. We used the National Gallery's 'Take one picture' and came up with lots of different activities. The children have been in their element as they can focus on their strongest intelligence and create an activity for their group. It has also given them the chance to improve their other intelligences as they could choose from the other activities once they had completed their own. Advice was given to their peers if they needed it. It has been a very successful week with lots of great work.

MI, real life and Critical Skills

One of the best educational packages around at the moment is the Critical Skills Programme, www.criticalskills.co.uk. It provides a perfect example of the 'authentic problems' MI pathway.

It all started in a bar one Friday evening. After the usual uphill five-day struggle, a group of New Hampshire teachers met to bemoan the sorry state of US education. President Reagan's 'A Nation at Risk' had just been published, and everyone was reeling from the shock: teachers were failing; schools disorganized; and students demotivated. Poor education had put the nation's future business prosperity at great risk. But instead of crying into their beer, these teachers ordered another round and faced up to the challenges.

After a few hours chatting, they hit on an idea. They agreed to meet again the following week, but this time each of them would bring a friend from the business world. Why? To find out what sort of people the business world expected kids to turn into.

From these two meetings a larger project emerged. Over the following summer vacation, the two groups – teachers and their business friends – met separately to think about the problem. The teachers set to work on a list of skills and attitudes which they wanted their students to develop – the talents and characteristics of effective learners. The other group asked a similar question of their employees: What qualities does a worker need to have? What characteristics make for strong, competitive businesses and help to ensure future prosperity?

When they'd finished, they compared notes and surprise, surprise the two lists were virtually identical: organization, leadership, communication, critical thinking, creative thinking and ten others. They concluded that school and business both wanted the same things. So why not start teaching them from the first day at school?

That's just what happened and several years later, the Critical Skills Programme was born. It used the best methods to teach not only the basics (literacy, numeracy, ICT), but also the skills and qualities needed to be effective at work. Failing schools with huge vandalism bills, drug and gun problems embraced the programme and saw astonishing results. Students became responsible for their own learning and approached it with a spirit of enterprise. The programme valued their personal qualities, so they began to value their learning.

In 1999, the Critical Skills Programme (CSP) came to the UK and since then it has transformed the school lives of many children. Over 3,000 teachers have been trained in many parts of the country – Bradford, South Wales, Bristol, West Lothian, and in Jersey it's now a requirement that any teacher coming to work in an island school must complete a CSP course as part of their induction. The late, and greatly missed Ted Wragg, professor of education at Exeter University, evaluated the programme and gave it top marks. And under his guidance, Talkback TV produced an acclaimed series of programmes called *The Unteachables* where CSP was featured.

The Critical Skills identified by the programme are:

- Organization
- Leadership
- Management
- Problem solving

- Decision making
- Critical thinking
- Creative thinking
- Communication.

And the Fundamental Dispositions (ways of behaving/charactistics):

- Lifelong learner
- Quality worker
- Self-directed
- Ethical character

- Collaboration
- Curiosity/wonder
- Community member.

CSP provides a coherent framework for the best teaching methods and tools through its experiential cycle.

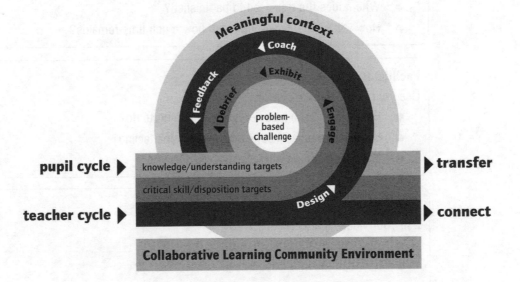

Two key themes of the programme are:

1. Building a collaborative learning community.

2. Using experiential, problem-based challenges to delivering curriculum content while at the same time developing the Critical Skills and Fundamental Dispositions.

Multiple intelligences theory and practice has a big part to play in both.

Communities are built from individuals and their links with each other. An effective community is made by:

- recognizing, valuing and using individual talents

- developing strong relationships between individuals and in groups.

Multiple intelligences profiling identifies talents so that they can be shared and used.

The Critical Skills Programme creates and maintains learning communities by using community-building activities and small group-work. In the community-building activities, everyone is involved in solving short puzzles, taking part in challenges and playing games. Small group-work is founded on the concept of 'group roles' – group management responsibilities shared out between members.

In small groups, learners will find all the skills necessary to complete most tasks – and tasks that no single learner could complete in the same time frame. Below are six roles, based on MI skills, which make for an effective small group.

Roles in a Critical Skills small group

Timekeeper

Use your logical/mathematical skills.

- How long do you have for the task?
- When does the task need to be finished?
- How will you let the group know how much time remains?

Facilitator

Use your interpersonal skills.

- Does every team member have something to do?
- Has everyone had a say? How is everyone feeling?
- Is the team doing what it's supposed to?

Artist

Use your visual/spatial skills.

- What information do you need to present?
- How can the information be presented clearly?
- What colours/style/design will suit the information?

Reporter

Use your verbal/linguistic skills.

- What needs writing and saying?
- What form does the writing/speaking take?
- What are the needs of the audience?

Builder

Use your bodily/kinesthetic skills.

- What needs making/moving/fixing/getting?
- Do you have the tools and materials that the group will need?
- Is your work area well organized?

Checker

Use your logical/mathematical skills.

- Is the group doing what it has been asked to do?
- Are all success criteria being met?
- Is the team collaborating effectively and efficiently?

Some tasks may require different, more specialized skills (music, for example). In this case, the teacher's and learners' MI knowledge can help in assembling groups with the right mix of abilities. And the same individuals can reform in response to different jobs.

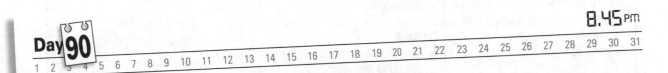

Day 90   8.45 PM

I had a visitor today from a primary school in the Isle of Wight. The teacher wanted to find out more about multiple intelligences and what different schools are doing. I felt quite privileged but also a little nervous as the class were not yet working in their MI groups as was planned.

In the Critical Skills Programme, curriculum content is delivered in ways that emulate workplace projects: outcomes are negotiated, project groups formed, timescales agreed and resources identified. Frequently, students are cast in real-life roles – artist, businessman, designer, architect, publisher, and sometimes the real thing (an artist, businesswoman and so on) is invited into school to evaluate students' work.

The projects are called 'challenges'. They replace lesson plans, but do exactly the same job. They express learning objectives, success criteria and target skills.

The Critical Skills challenge for secondary English given on the following page was written by Margaret Goodwin, a teacher and Critical Skills trainer. The end product of a challenge – what students make to demonstrate their learning – can be any number of things. In this challenge it's a playscript, but it could be a diagram, audio recording or poster.

Essential knowledge/question: How could we adapt *A Midsummer Night's Dream* as a puppet show for seven year olds?		
Challenge	**Product criteria (rule, form and content)**	**Process criteria (skills and/or dispositions)**
Many of you will have seen a Punch and Judy show, if not in real life then on television. It makes use of hand puppets to tell a story. *A Midsummer Night's Dream* contains many characters and a potentially confusing storyline. Your challenge is to simplify the play for a young audience and to present it using hand or finger puppets. In groups of four, choose key characters and rewrite the play to make it as simple as possible. Make suitable puppets and design a set in preparation for presenting your version to a group of seven year olds.	**Rules** • Work in teams of four. • Complete your work in five lessons. • Include all members in your play. **Form** • Write a playscript that is correctly laid out and includes stage directions. **Content** • Your script must contain the essential storyline of *A Midsummer Night's Dream*. **Performance** • All team members must participate and provide dialogue, puppets provide the actions. • A suitable set must be produced. • The plot must be made clear to the audience. • The dialogue must be clearly audible.	**Knowledge** Listen for reference to key characters by name and the part played in the plot. **Skill** Quality conversation

Different products call for different talents, and Critical Skills teachers are able to match type of product to student needs (because they have taken the time to build their learning community). A class or group MI profile tells you what they will be good at making, but also what will challenge them – a song may suit a musical group, but not a logical one.

Here is a list of products suggested by the intelligences:

Intelligence	Example of assessment product
Musical	Song, opera, pop record, close harmony, musical, jingle
Linguistic	Essay, poem, interview, review, phone call, email exchange
Naturalist	Hierarchy, taxonomy, classification, key, diorama
Interpersonal	Group presentation, committee meeting, team strategy/tactic
Intrapersonal	Diary, monologue, explorer's journal, guided meditation
Visual	Live webcam, 3D model, painting, video, diagram, mind map
Mathematical	Flow chart, Venn diagram, calculation, experiment, concept map
Bodily	Dance, role play, frieze, puppet show, mime

Field trips and school visits

A day out can be the highlight of the term for many children. Residential stays, field trips and exchange visits all make a welcome change to the classroom, but often the trip itself is the focus, not the learning.

MI can provide a structure for getting more out of school visits. In this example of a Year 9 visit to a local church, MI has been used to create five expert groups, each with a role and task. For more groups you could include other intelligences, but you don't have to use all of them all of the time.

Intelligence	Role	Task: find and record evidence of...
Musical	A team of music producers	...music in the church, then plan a CD to sum up the building (the tracks will be recorded live in the church).
Linguistic	A team of linguists	...languages in the church and how language is used.
Visual	A team of visual installation artists	...visual artwork in the church. Plan a new piece of installation art that synthesizes elements from these pieces.
Existential	A team of philosophers	... religious, philosophical and spiritual practices in the church. Produce an objective summary of what people coming to this church believe.
Interpersonal/ Intrapersonal	A team of sociologists	...what people do in the church and why. Produce a role play showing how people behave in and out of church.

This method can be used with other trips and visits. All you have to do is:

- cast individuals and groups in real-life roles
- allocate genuine tasks related to the roles
- ask groups to present their work to each other.

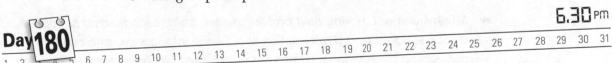

6.30 pm

Day 180

1 2 3 4 5 6 7 8 9 10 11 12 13 14 15 16 17 18 19 20 21 22 23 24 25 26 27 28 29 30 31

What a relief. Nearly all over for another year. It's been a good year. Busy at the start as we had to learn about the intelligences, think up new activities, sort out displays. I've seen a huge rise in the children's esteem and confidence (in themselves and each other). It was a real awe-and-wonder moment when they all knew that no one was more intelligent than anyone else. I couldn't say this had any immediate effect on progress, as so many of the tests are linguistic (and so don't cater for all those other intelligences!). Still, who knows, maybe this is going to change!

Putting it all together

This handbook is full of 'how to's – how to think, teach and learn with MI. Exactly how you use the ideas depends on your circumstances. To reiterate what's possible, let's finish with inspirational descriptions from three schools that have committed to MI in a big way – one primary and one secondary in the UK – and one in the USA.

Case study

Resource: Whole-school implementation of MI, primary
Teacher: Louise Rich, assistant deputy head
Location: Wallisdean Junior School, Fareham

Wallisdean Junior has 225 children, including seven who receive support through the Resourced Provision for Deaf Children. The school is in an area of some social deprivation, with approximately 25 per cent of pupils on the SEN register.

Among other things, Louise Rich is responsible for turning 'learning theory' into 'learning practice'. Most recently, she has focused on the school's implementation of multiple intelligences.

'I first became interested in MI after attending a "thinking" course in 2001. I was able to put MI theory into practice through action research with a Year 6 class over a year. Since then, MI has been high profile for the whole school. Having shared ideas with colleagues about celebrating, matching and stretching, and agreeing the terminology we would use, we decided to concentrate on "celebrating" as a crucial means of boosting self-esteem and self-belief.

'With the standards agenda focusing on English, maths and science, we were determined children would not feel they had failed if they performed badly in these. We wanted them to recognize their own and each other's intelligence and that all intelligences are equally valued. With celebrating in mind, we set up the following:

- *MI environment. Having built profiles of each child, each teacher set up MI displays. Some put up information about each intelligence, with children's names and photographs. Others set up different MI zones, such as an interpersonal zone with friendship beanbags. There is a display of intelligences in the main entrance, updated regularly with work from MI activities.*

- *MI activities. Following all teachers and LSAs finding out their own MI profiles, staff planned MI activities. Teachers and LSAs work with a group of children across the year groups who share similar strengths. The art-clever staff and children worked on a project on Van Gogh, while the body-clever team learned juggling and circus tricks! At the moment, activity sessions are held half-termly and children go to different sessions because they are good at more than one thing, so avoiding labelling.*

- *MI clubs. The gardening club have grown amazing sunflowers and organic vegetables and the craft club made wonderful Christmas decorations. We have managed to run clubs for all intelligences at some point in the year and the planned Scrabble and philosophy clubs hope to tweak the buttons* of the word-clever and self-clever children this term. We also try to get a balance of visitors in school, such as theatre groups and musicians.

- *MI magazine. We are about to launch our first MI magazine. Interpersonal children will run the problem page, art-clever children will produce the cover and pictures and body-clever children will contribute sports reports.*

- *MI mural. The first thing seen entering the school grounds is a huge MI mural. The designs were done by the children and, with the help of a local artist, they created the mural from broken tiles. It's an excellent focal point and gives a strong message that we are all clever in different ways.*

- *MI celebrations. We give out certificates in a weekly assembly for children who have excelled in a particular intelligence, reinforcing that each intelligence is equally valued. Some classes have recently started linking good behaviour with MI reward time.*

Case study

Resource: Whole-school implementation of MI, secondary
Teacher: Jo Iles, learning to learn gateway leader
Location: Gillotts School, Henley-on-Thames

Gillotts is an 11–16 comprehensive with 890 students. In 2005, 72 per cent of students gained 5 A*–C passes. It is a Maths and Computing Specialist School.

In September 2005, the school was restructured using David Hargreaves' nine 'gateways to learning' as a focus. The school sees the personalized learning agenda as key – each student becoming responsible for his or her own learning and being equipped with the tools to improve.

Jo Iles has been teaching English and media studies at Gillotts for four years. She is responsible for managing the learning to learn gateway across the school.

Jo made MI the first area to focus on 'because it is child-centred: making them aware of how they are clever, thus raising self-esteem and self-confidence. I felt this was an important step towards children seeing themselves at the centre of their own learning, encouraging ownership and independence.' She introduced the following steps:

- *MI with staff. Jo gave a presentation on MI to all teaching staff, from which they completed their own profiles.*

- *MI with tutor groups. In the first term, tutors led a session in which they challenged students' perceptions of intelligence by asking questions such as, 'Who is more intelligent – David Beckham or the Dalai Lama?' Students' own MI profiles are displayed in their learning files, accessible to students, parents and teachers.*

- *MI with parents. Parents and carers have a vital role in children becoming independent learners. At parents' information evenings for Years 7 and 10, Jo introduced the concepts of learning to learn and MI. Parents were encouraged to identify their MI profile and use this in talking with their children about how they could support them in their learning.*

- *MI in Year 7. Year 7 students now have one learning to learn lesson per fortnight. These are led by a small team of specialist teachers, and include brain theory, MI, emotional intelligence and thinking skills.*

- *MI across the curriculum. Following training, all staff include opportunities for students to demonstrate their learning through the different intelligences. A lesson-planning pro forma has been developed to aid this.*

- *MI research. Through the Specialist Schools and Academies Trust, the school is now leading a network of schools that share experiences and develop learning to learn in all subjects.*

Soon after I discovered MI, I discovered New City School in St Louis – one of the first 'MI schools'. I am indebted to Portsmouth City Council and specifically the then CEO, John Gaskin, for sponsoring my trip. The following is from my visit report, showing another way of putting our MI learning together.

I'm meeting New City School's director, Tom Hoerr. Tom has worked closely with Howard Gardner, who has been tracking his theory in Tom's school and stops by from time to time.

New City School began its MI journey in 1988 after a series of faculty reading sessions. They took a chapter a week from *Frames of Mind* and now the school is a world leader. I step in the door and am greeted by a Driffon. This papier mâché dragon-griffon has eight heads, one for each intelligence. Tom prides himself that each child in the school contributed to it in some way. The linguistic head is covered in letters, the musical one in notes. A new beast or additional heads will be needed as Gardner expands his theory.

I start my tour with Sheryl Reardon's 2nd Grade children (equivalent to Year 3), who are practising cursive handwriting. The classroom is calm, quiet and well equipped, with a mezzanine floor holding books and an armchair. There's no obvious evidence of MI here until Sheryl tells me that the children are all familiar with their profiles, and Bret, the class greeter, shows me his profile folder.

After recess, I watch the 5th Grade (Year 6) rehearse for their end-of-year performance in the Founders Hall. They've been to the Civil Rights Museum in Memphis. Each of the three classes contribute. The last group challenges the audience to address race issues. This is a brave piece, sensitively and proactively preparing the children for life in a multiracial society. The walls of the Hall are filled with quotes and inspirational words. Next to a picture of Tom, I read some words I have by my own desk, 'It's our choices make us what we are Harry, more than our abilities,' from *Harry Potter and the Philosopher's Stone*.

Later, in another 5th Grade room, I watch children make their end-of-term wall presentations. The floor is a chaos of paper, card, paint and glue and everyone is engaged with their work. Hannah explains her approach: 'I'm visual and BK, so I've got lots of pictures, and I made this background pattern.' The theme is 'Things that make a difference'. Hannah has used her bodily intelligence by including icons of technological development, in the form of a 3D model fixed on a twentieth-century timeline.

Children who have finished are in the book area, absorbed in their reading. The teacher, Chris Hass, is free to guide individuals in self-reflection – another cornerstone of New City's model. He's working at the PC with a student. He tells me that valuing children's stronger intelligences helps him to boost their weaker ones. He points to some work on fighter aircraft. The boy working on it is behind in writing, and his work reflects this – all pictures, guided by his major intelligence. But there is a carefully written and constructed true/false section. That might not be there if it were the only method of expression permitted.

Librarian Joe Corbett isn't class based. Each group of children visits him weekly for library instruction. He reads stories like a professional broadcaster and the 2nd Grade children are captivated.

The kindergarten is multilevel, bright, noisy, stimulating and busy. Stairs, corners, turrets and doors make this a learning wonderland. Teacher Monette Gooch-Smith is an MI veteran who runs her own workshops across America. She tells me there are 24 learning areas in kindergarten, each addressing a different combination of intelligences. She gives me an example: Rachael is strongly naturalist and visual. Last week, she planned and led the class on a nature walk and got her colleagues to paint something they found on the trip. Remember, this girl is six years old.

Monette explains how children are naturally tuned to their strengths, and how teachers are not always receptive. She acts out a young girl trying to learn: 'The teacher is talking, talking, talking. The girl starts to move, thinking, "I need BK here." Teacher says, "Keep still." "Ah ha," thinks the girl, "let's try visual." She starts to doodle about what the teacher's saying. "Stop drawing," says the teacher. The girl thinks, "Let's try interpersonal," so she whispers a question to her friend. "Stop talking," says the teacher...' I have great difficulty leaving this learning heaven...

Tom invites me to dinner. Five New City teachers join us and Tom gets me to share the tale of how I came to visit the States. The teachers are impressed at Portsmouth's forward thinking. Of his 700 visitors a year, Tom can't recall the last one from the UK. The meal has the feel of a family gathering – Tom heading the table, his children home for the weekend. Tom stresses collegiality as a necessary foundation to developing MI (or any other) theory school-wide. And he certainly has it here.

The teachers discuss their end-of-year reports and tease Tom about the workload. He acknowledges it's tough. The talk turns to children. These educators show an enviable fondness for their students and for Tom. And they praise the children's concern for each other: 'Sure, they'll challenge you, but they never make fun of each other. Differences are for celebrating not exploiting.'

From five years old, New City students know they are uniquely intelligent. From then on, issues of race or size or hair colour are simply further confirmation of each person's specialness.

I've dedicated an area of my website to MI: www.thinkingclassroom.co.uk. You'll find additional resources, clips from Natalie's video diary, and web links. Please email mike@aspiroweb.co.uk with any MI-related questions, comments or ideas.

Thank you for reading, and remember:

'There are hundreds and hundreds of ways to succeed and many many different abilities that will help you get there.'

Howard Gardner

resources

Photocopiable resources

How are you clever?

Name: _____   Date: _____

Colour in the box next to each statement if you agree with it.
If you 'sort of' agree, colour in half of the box.
If you disagree, leave the box empty.
The more colour there is for an intelligence, the stronger that intelligence may be for you.

Linguistic		I enjoy reading.
		I enjoy listening to the radio.
		I can talk my way out of trouble.
		I can persuade my parents to do things.
		I sometimes get into trouble at school for talking too much.
Logical		I can do maths in my head easily.
		I can spot mistakes easily.
		I enjoy playing games like Cluedo or chess.
		I like to plan ahead.
		I sometimes get into trouble at school for arguing.
Visual		I can picture things in my head easily.
		I enjoy doing jigsaw puzzles.
		I am good at following maps.
		I like to draw or doodle.
		I sometimes get into trouble at school for daydreaming.
Bodily		I enjoy sport or physical activity.
		I like working with my hands.
		I sometimes get into trouble at school for not sitting still.
		I need to touch things to learn more about them.
		I use my hands when I talk.
Musical		I like singing.
		I tap my fingers/feet when I hear music.
		I listen to music a lot.
		I sometimes get into trouble at school for humming/tapping the table.
		I hum/sing while I'm working.
Interpersonal		I am good at working out how other people feel.
		I like working in a team.
		When I have a problem, I ask someone for help.
		I sometimes get into trouble for talking about what I've been up to outside school.
		I like to go out.
Intrapersonal		I like working on my own.
		I sometimes get into trouble at school for not taking part.
		I know what I'm good at.
		I know what I want to do when I grow up.
		When I have a problem, I sort it myself.
Naturalist		I enjoy spending time outside.
		I can name many plants/animals.
		I enjoy playing in my garden or in the park.
		I sometimes get into trouble at school for staring out of the window.
		My family has a pet and I enjoy caring for it.
Existential		I go to church/mosque/temple/synagogue.
		I sometimes get into trouble at school for asking difficult questions.
		I am interested in new ideas.
		I pray now and again/regularly.
		I spend lots of time just thinking about things.

Multiple Intelligences in Practice © Mike Fleetham (Network Continuum, 2006)

How are you clever?

Name: _____   Date: _____

Colour in the circle for things you do a lot or enjoy.
If you 'sort of' enjoy it, or do it a little, colour in half the circle.
If you don't enjoy it or don't do it, leave the circle empty.
The more colour there is for an intelligence, the stronger that intelligence may be for you.

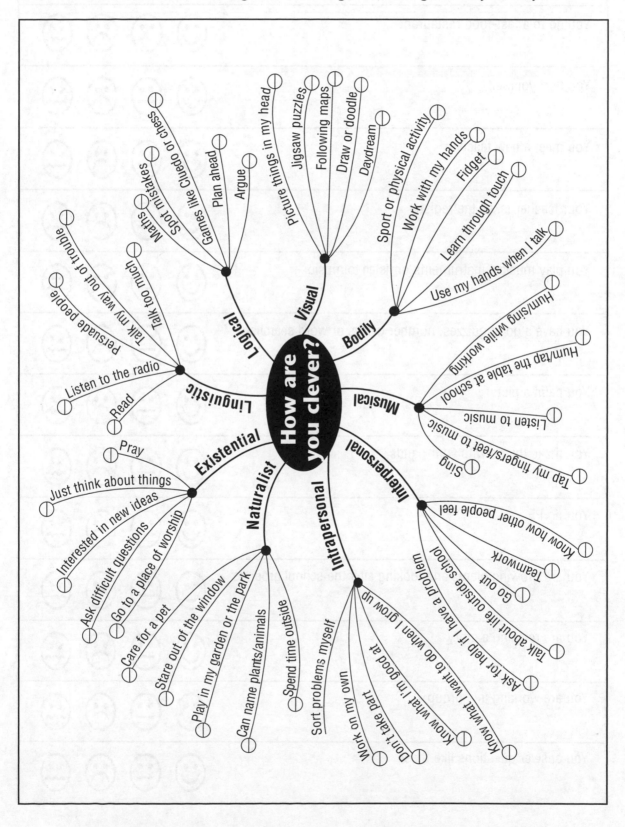

MI through feelings questionnaire

Name: _____   Date: _____

How do you feel when...				
You go to a fast-food restaurant	😊	😐	☹️	😖
You hurt yourself	😊	😐	☹️	😖
You meet a new teacher	😊	😐	☹️	😖
Your teacher takes the register	😊	😐	☹️	😖
You play musical instruments or listen to music	😊	😐	☹️	😖
You have a go at quizzes, number games or word searches	😊	😐	☹️	😖
You paint a picture	😊	😐	☹️	😖
You make things with your hands	😊	😐	☹️	😖
You do PE	😊	😐	☹️	😖
You are growing plants and looking after the school grounds	😊	😐	☹️	😖
You are retelling a story	😊	😐	☹️	😖
You are working in a group	😊	😐	☹️	😖
You answer questions like these	😊	😐	☹️	😖

Visual MI questionnaire

Name: _____ Date: _____

1. Child(ren) painting **Visual/kinesthetic**	**2.** A Big Book **Linguistic**	**3.** Children sitting talking **Interpersonal**	**4.** Children watching a DVD **Visual**
5. Child(ren) making things with clay/plasticine **Kinesthetic**	**6.** Child(ren) making D&T models **Kinesthetic**	**7.** D&T models on display **Visual/kinesthetic**	**8.** Children dancing together **Kinesthetic/ interpersonal**
9. Child(ren) gardening **Naturalist**	**10.** Low gym equipment **Kinesthetic**	**11.** Child(ren) doing jigsaws **Visual/kinesthetic**	**12.** Child(ren) in the library **Linguistic**
13. Child(ren) handling maths equipment **Logial/kinesthetic**	**14.** Child(ren) playing instruments **Musical**	**15.** Pair of children playing together in playground **Naturalist/ interpersonal**	**16.** Group of children playing together in playground **Naturalist/ interpersonal**
17. Pair of children at computer, talking **Logical/linguistic**	**18.** Child(ren) listening to CD **Musical**	**19.** Child working alone **Intrapersonal**	**20.** Child playing alone **Intrapersonal**
21. Child looking through magnifying glass **Logical**	**22.** Child listening to spoken word tape, wearing headphones **Linguistic**	Comments	

Student observations

Name: _____

Note the date under the behaviour when observed. Add your own observations as appropriate.

Musical/rhythmic

Moves in response to music that has a distinct beat	Hums, sings, taps while working	Sings in the playground		

Verbal/linguistic

Listens carefully for long periods with genuine understanding	Talks during 'quiet time'	Hands in unsolicited six-page stories written over the weekend		

Existential

Asks why and how	Gives 'off the wall' answers	Shows an interest in religions		

Naturalist

Chooses animal books – fiction/non-fiction	Looks out through the classroom window	Enjoys the curriculum content of a school trip		

Interpersonal

Has several stable, long-term friendships	Discusses life outside school with friends	Works effectively with others – leads		

Intrapersonal

Shows self-knowledge, e.g. 'I'm the sort of person who…'	Chooses to work alone	Works effectively alone		

Visual/spatial

Doodles	Daydreams	Makes accurate real-life pictures		

Logical/mathematical

Needs to be organized and neat when working	Asks for reasons	Excels in problem solving		

Bodily/kinesthetic

Uses hands when talking	Gets out of seat when not supposed to	Catches a ball consistently		

Multiple Intelligences in Practice © Mike Fleetham (Network Continuum, 2006)

MI-based parents' meeting

Child: _____   Date: _____

Parents: _____

Record parent responses to these questions, and others you might add, under the relevant intelligence below.

- What does s/he enjoy doing?
- What is s/he good at?
- What does s/he avoid doing?
- What is his/her favourite subject at school?

- What is his/her least favourite subject at school?
- What does s/he choose to do in spare time?
- What hobbies does s/he have?
- What would s/he like to be when grown up?

Verbal/linguistic
Mathematical/logical
Musical/rhythmic
Visual/spatial
Bodily/kinesthetic
Interpersonal
Intrapersonal
Naturalist

How are you clever? (Parent's/carer's version)

Name: _____   Date: _____

Shade in the box next to each statement if you agree with it.
If you partly agree, shade in half of the box.
If you disagree, leave the box empty.
The more shading there is for an intelligence, the stronger that intelligence may be for you.

Linguistic		I enjoy reading.
		I enjoy listening to the radio.
		I can talk my way out of trouble.
		I can persuade my partner/friends/colleagues to do things.
		I sometimes got into trouble at school for talking too much.
Logical		I can do maths in my head easily.
		I can easily spot the flaws in people reasoning.
		I enjoy playing games like Cluedo or chess.
		I like to plan ahead.
		I sometimes got into trouble at school for arguing.
Visual		I can picture things in my head easily.
		I enjoy doing jigsaw puzzles.
		I am good at reading maps.
		I like to draw or doodle.
		I sometimes got into trouble at school for daydreaming.
Bodily		I enjoy playing sport or doing physical activities.
		I like working with my hands.
		I sometimes got into trouble at school for not sitting still.
		I need to touch things to learn more about them.
		I use my hands when I talk.
Musical		I like singing.
		I tap my fingers/feet when I hear music.
		I listen to music a lot.
		I sometimes got into trouble at school for humming/tapping the table.
		I hum/sing while I'm working or doing chores.
Interpersonal		I am good at working out how other people feel.
		I like working in a team.
		When I have a problem, I ask someone for help.
		I sometimes got into trouble for talking about what I'd been up to outside school.
		I have a good social life and lots of friends.
Intrapersonal		I like working on my own.
		I sometimes got into trouble at school for not taking part.
		I know what I'm good at.
		I'm into personal development.
		When I have a problem, I sort it myself.
Naturalist		I enjoy spending time outside.
		I can name many plants/animals.
		I enjoy gardening.
		I sometimes got into trouble at school for staring out of the window.
		We have a pet and I enjoy caring for it.
Existential		I go to church/mosque/temple/synagogue.
		I sometimes got into trouble at school for asking difficult questions.
		I am interested in new ideas.
		I pray now and again/regularly.
		I sometimes spend time just thinking about things.

Multiple Intelligences in Practice © Mike Fleetham (Network Continuum, 2006)

Further reading and resources

Most MI resources come from America and relate to its educational system (though I heard recently that there are over 100 books in Chinese about MI). It is good stuff, but it does need translating to the current UK situation. With quality rather than quantity in mind, here are a small number of well-chosen sources of further information.

Books

Howard Gardner's *Frames of Mind* (Basic Books) is the definitive text for MI theory. In 1999 he published *Intelligence Reframed* (Basic Books) – an update written in light of experience. This second book is a very useful read because Gardner explores the diverse ways in which his work has been interpreted – not always in line with his original intentions. He also argues clearly and effectively against his critics and includes case studies and anecdotes from around the world. He takes the opportunity to counter the many myths and misinterpretations that have grown up around his ideas. Neither book comes with a set of classroom ideas, but both give you a strong foundation for using MI and make useful allies if anyone wants to know what you're up to (and why!).

Another recent book that looks at the application of MI in the primary classroom is *Multiple Intelligences in the Elementary Classroom: A Teacher's Toolkit* by Susan Baum, Julie Viens and Barbara Slatin (Teachers College Press).

Becoming a Multiple Intelligences School by Tom Hoerr (ASCD) is an inspirational source of ideas for putting the theory into whole-school practice.

The Association for Supervision and Curriculum Development is a worldwide community of educators advocating sound policies and sharing best practices to achieve the success of each learner. To learn more, visit ASCD at www.ascd.org.

Internet

A great place to begin your surfing is New Horizons for Learning at www.newhorizons.org/strategies/mi/front_mi.htm. After a brief introduction you'll find links to over 25 online articles and loads of further reading.

Tom Hoerr also sends out a free MI e-newsletter through ASCD. Contact Tom at: trhoerr@newcityschool.org.

If you want something a bit more interactive online, http://groups.yahoo.com/group/M-I will get you to a useful but not very active discussion group.

An area of my website – www.thinkingclassroom.co.uk – has further MI resources and links. Contact: mike@aspiroweb.co.uk.

Video, audio and CD-ROM

The ASCD also produces MI learning resources. Visit www.ascd.org and select 'Education Topics', then 'Multiple Intelligences'. Look at 'Resources' to see what's available.

Further resources listed by chapter

Section 1: Discovering MI
Personalized learning
For more information about personalized learning, get a copy of *Personalising learning: Next steps in working laterally* by David Hargreaves (iNET). The first chapter can be downloaded free from: www.schoolsnetwork.org.uk/content/articles/3292/chapt1nextsteps.pdf.

Also visit www.everychildmatters.gov.uk/ete/personalisedlearning.

MI, IQ and g
Intelligence – A Very Short Introduction by Ian J. Deary (OUP)

'Multiple Intelligences, Curriculum and Assessment Project, Final Report' by Áine Hyland, University College Cork, 2000

Eight and a half ways to be clever
For technical information on the visual intelligence, see Visual *Intelligence: How We Create What We See* by Donald D. Hoffman (W.W. Norton & Co).

For practice in the musical intelligence, combined with bodily/ kinesthetic, visit www.voicetraining.co.uk.

For training, products and quizzes to improve teaching and learning through emotional intelligence, browse the Discovery Project's site at www.discovery-project.com.

Section 2: Using MI

Stage 3: How to understand MI

The Birmingham Grid for Learning MI Wheel:
www.bgfl.org/multipleintelligences.

MIDAS profiling: www.miresearch.org/onlineassessment.php.

Howard Gardner's Spectrum project:
http://pzweb.harvard.edu/Research/Spectrum.htm.

The MEDIATE profile room research project:
www.port.ac.uk/research/mediate.

Stage 4: How to create an MI environment

How to Create and Develop a Thinking Classroom by Mike Fleetham (LDA)

For some multiple intelligences posters for display, try:
   Key Stage 1 – www.networkpress.co.uk/MI_KS1.html
   Key Stage 2 – www.aspiroweb.co.uk/multipleintelligences/posters.asp
   Key Stages 2–4 – www.networkpress.co.uk/MI_KS2-4.html.

Stage 5: How to teach and learn with MI

Specialist Schools and Academies Trust: www.specialistschools.org.uk.

Critical Skills Programme: www.criticalskills.co.uk.

Index

Other titles from Network Continuum Education

ACCELERATED LEARNING SERIES

Accelerated Learning: A User's Guide by Alistair Smith, Mark Lovatt & Derek Wise
Accelerated Learning in the Classroom by Alistair Smith
Accelerated Learning in Practice by Alistair Smith
The ALPS Approach: Accelerated Learning in Primary Schools by Alistair Smith & Nicola Call
The ALPS Approach Resource Book by Alistair Smith & Nicola Call
MapWise by Oliver Caviglioli & Ian Harris
Creating an Accelerated Learning School by Mark Lovatt & Derek Wise
Thinking for Learning by Mel Rockett & Simon Percival
Reaching out to all learners by Cheshire LEA
Move It: Physical movement and learning by Alistair Smith
Coaching Solutions by Will Thomas & Alistair Smith
Coaching Solutions Resource Book by Will Thomas

ABLE AND TALENTED CHILDREN COLLECTION

Effective Provision for Able and Talented Children by Barry Teare
Effective Resources for Able and Talented Children by Barry Teare
More Effective Resources for Able and Talented Children by Barry Teare
Challenging Resources for Able and Talented Children by Barry Teare
Enrichment Activities for Able and Talented Children by Barry Teare
Parents' and Carers' Guide for Able and Talented Children by Barry Teare

LEARNING TO LEARN

The Practical Guide to Revision Techniques by Simon Percival
Let's Learn How to Learn: Workshops for Key Stage 2 by UFA National Team
Brain Friendly Revision by UFA National Team
Learning to Learn for Life: research and practical examples for Foundation Stage and Key
   Stage 1 by Rebecca Goodbourn, Susie Parsons, Julia Wright, Steve Higgins & Kate Wall
Creating a Learning to Learn School by Toby Greany & Jill Rodd
Teaching Pupils How to Learn by Bill Lucas, Toby Greany, Jill Rodd & Ray Wicks

EXCITING ICT

New Tools for Learning: Accelerated Learning meets ICT by John Davitt
Creative ICT in the Classroom: Using new tools for learning by the Learning Discovery Centre Team
Exciting ICT in Maths by Alison Clark-Jeavons
Exciting ICT in English by Tony Archdeacon
Exciting ICT in History by Ben Walsh

PRIMARY RESOURCES

Foundations of Literacy by Sue Palmer & Ros Bayley
Flying Start with Literacy by Ros Bayley
The Thinking Child by Nicola Call with Sally Featherstone
The Thinking Child Resource Book by Nicola Call with Sally Featherstone
Critical Skills in the Early Years by Vicki Charlesworth

Towards Successful Learning by Diana Pardoe
But Why? Developing philosophical thinking in the classroom by Sara Stanley with Steve Bowkett
Help Your Child To Succeed by Bill Lucas & Alistair Smith
Help Your Child To Succeed – Toolkit by Bill Lucas & Alistair Smith
Promoting Children's Well-Being in the Primary Years:
    The Right from the Start Handbook edited by Andrew Burrell & Jeni Riley
Numeracy Activities Key Stage 2 by Afzal Ahmed & Honor Williams
Numeracy Activities Key Stage 3 by Afzal Ahmed, Honor Williams & George Wickham

LEARNING THROUGH SONGS
That's English! Learning English through songs (Key Stage 2) by Tim Harding
That's Maths! Learning maths through songs (Key Stage 2) by Tim Harding
Maths in Action! Learning maths through music & animation – interactive CD-ROM
    (Key Stage 2) by Tim Harding
That's Science! Learning science through songs (Key Stage 2) by Tim Harding
This is Science! Learning science through songs and stories (Key Stage 1) by Tim Harding

VISUAL LEARNING
Seeing History: Visual learning strategies & resources for Key Stage 3 by Tom Haward
Reaching out to all thinkers by Ian Harris & Oliver Caviglioli
Think it–Map it! by Ian Harris & Oliver Caviglioli
Thinking Skills & Eye Q by Oliver Caviglioli, Ian Harris & Bill Tindall

DISPLAY MATERIAL
Bright Sparks by Alistair Smith
More Bright Sparks by Alistair Smith
Leading Learning by Alistair Smith
Move It posters: Physical movement and learning by Alistair Smith
Multiple Intelligence Posters (KS1 and KS2–4) edited by Alistair Smith
Emotional Intelligence Posters (KS1 and KS2–4) edited by Alistair Smith
Thinking Skills & Eye Q posters by Oliver Caviglioli, Ian Harris & Bill Tindall

EMOTIONAL INTELLIGENCE
Moving to Secondary School by Lynda Measor with Mike Fleetham
Future Directions by Diane Carrington and Helen Whitten
Tooncards: A multi-purpose resource for developing communication skills by Chris Terrell
Becoming Emotionally Intelligent by Catherine Corrie
Lend Us Your Ears by Rosemary Sage
Class Talk by Rosemary Sage
A World of Difference by Rosemary Sage
Best behaviour and Best behaviour FIRST AID
    by Peter Relf, Rod Hirst, Jan Richardson & Georgina Youdell
    Best behaviour FIRST AID also available separately
Self-Intelligence by Stephen Bowkett
Imagine That... by Stephen Bowkett
ALPS StoryMaker by Stephen Bowkett
StoryMaker Catch Pack by Stephen Bowkett
With Drama in Mind by Patrice Baldwin

PERSONALIZING LEARNING

Personalizing Learning: Transforming education for every child by John West-Burnham & Max Coates

Transforming education for every child: A practical handbook by John West-Burnham & Max Coates

Personalizing Learning in the 21st Century edited by Sara de Freitas & Chris Yapp

The Power of Diversity by Barbara Prashnig

Learning Styles in Action by Barbara Prashnig

EFFECTIVE LEARNING & LEADERSHIP

Effective Heads of Department by Phil Jones & Nick Sparks

Leading the Learning School by Colin Weatherley

Transforming Teaching & Learning by Colin Weatherley with Bruce Bonney, John Kerr & Jo Morrison

Classroom Management by Philip Waterhouse & Chris Dickinson

Effective Learning Activities by Chris Dickinson

Making Pupil Data Powerful by Maggie Pringle & Tony Cobb

Raising Boys' Achievement by Jon Pickering

Getting Started by Henry Liebling

Closing the Learning Gap by Mike Hughes

Strategies for Closing the Learning Gap by Mike Hughes with Andy Vass

Tweak to Transform by Mike Hughes

Lessons are for Learning by Mike Hughes

Nurturing Independent Thinkers edited by Mike Bosher & Patrick Hazlewood

Effective Teachers by Tony Swainston

Effective Teachers in Primary Schools by Tony Swainston

Effective Leadership in Schools by Tony Swainston

Leading Change in Schools: A Practical Handbook by Sian Case

VISIONS OF EDUCATION SERIES

Discover Your Hidden Talents: The essential guide to lifelong learning by Bill Lucas

The Brain's Behind It by Alistair Smith

Wise Up by Guy Claxton

The Unfinished Revolution by John Abbott & Terry Ryan

The Learning Revolution by Gordon Dryden & Jeannette Vos

SCHOOL GOVERNORS

Questions School Governors Ask by Joan Sallis

Basics for School Governors by Joan Sallis

The Effective School Governor by David Marriott (including audio tape)

For more information and ordering details, please consult our website
www.networkpress.co.uk

Network Continuum Education – much more than publishing...

Network Continuum Education Conferences – Invigorate your teaching

Each term NCE runs a wide range of conferences on cutting edge issues in teaching and learning at venues around the UK. The emphasis is always highly practical. Regular presenters include some of our top-selling authors such as Sue Palmer, Mike Hughes and Steve Bowkett. Dates and venues for our current programme of conferences can be found on our website www.networkpress.co.uk.

NCE online Learning Style Analysis – Find out how your students prefer to learn

Discovering what makes your students tick is the key to personalizing learning. NCE's Learning Style Analysis is a 50-question online evaluation that can give an immediate and thorough learning profile for every student in your class. It reveals how, when and where they learn best, whether they are right brain or left brain dominant, analytic or holistic, whether they are strongly auditory, visual, kinesthetic or tactile ... and a great deal more. And for teachers who'd like to take the next step, LSA enables you to create a whole-class profile for precision lesson planning.

Developed by The Creative Learning Company in New Zealand and based on the work of Learning Styles expert Barbara Prashnig, this powerful tool allows you to analyse your own and your students' learning preferences in a more detailed way than any other product we have ever seen. To find out more about Learning Style Analysis or to order profiles visit www.networkpress.co.uk/lsa.

Also available: Teaching Style Analysis and Working Style Analysis.

NCE's Critical Skills Programme – Teach your students skills for lifelong learning

The Critical Skills Programme puts pupils at the heart of learning, by providing the skills required to be successful in school and life. Classrooms are developed into effective learning environments, where pupils work collaboratively and feel safe enough to take 'learning risks'. Pupils have more ownership of their learning across the whole curriculum and are encouraged to develop not only subject knowledge but the fundamental skills of:

- problem solving
- creative thinking
- decision making
- communication
- management
- organization

- leadership
- self-direction
- quality working
- collaboration
- enterprise
- community involvement

"The Critical Skills Programme... energizes students to think in an enterprising way. CSP gets students to think for themselves, solve problems in teams, think outside the box, to work in a structured manner. CSP is the ideal way to forge an enterprising student culture."

Rick Lee, Deputy Director, Barrow Community Learning Partnership

To find out more about CSP training visit the Critical Skills Programme website at
www.criticalskills.co.uk